TAMING
YOUR INNER
Brat

W9-BZA-762

TAMING YOUR INNER Brat

A Guide for Transforming Self-Defeating Behavior

Pauline Wallin, PhD

ATRIA PAPERBACK
New York London Toronto Sydney New Delhi

BEYOND WORDS
Hillsboro, Oregon

ATRIA PAPERBACK
A Division of Simon & Schuster, Inc.
1230 Avenue of the Americas
New York, NY 10020

BEYOND WORDS
20827 N.W. Cornell Road, Suite 500
Hillsboro, Oregon 97124-9808
503-531-8700 / 503-531-8773 fax
www.beyondword.com

Copyright © 2001, 2004, 2011 by Pauline Wallin

Published in 2004 by Wildcat Canyon Press

All rights reserved, including the right to reproduce this book or portions thereof in any form whatsoever without the prior written permission of Atria Paperback/Beyond Words Publishing, Inc., except where permitted by law.

Managing editor: Julie Steigerwaldt
Editor: Carol Franks
Proofreader: Marvin Moore
Design: Janice Phelps / Peri Poloni
Composition: William H. Brunson Typography Services

First Atria Paperback/Beyond Words trade paperback edition 2011

ATRIA PAPERBACK and colophon are trademarks of Simon & Schuster, Inc. Beyond Words Publishing is an imprint of Simon & Schuster, Inc. and the Beyond Words logo is a registered trademark of Beyond Words Publishing, Inc.

For more information about special discounts for bulk purchases, please contact Simon & Schuster Special Sales at 1-866-506-1949 or business@simonandschuster.com.

The Simon & Schuster Speakers Bureau can bring authors to your live event. For more information or to book an event, contact the Simon & Schuster Speakers Bureau at 1-866-248-3049 or visit our website at www.simonspeakers.com.

Manufactured in the United States of America

10 9 8 7 6 5 4 3 2 1

Library of Congress Cataloging-in-Publication Data

Wallin, Pauline.
   Taming your inner brat : a guide for transforming self-defeating behavior / Pauline Wallin.
      p. cm.
Includes bibliographical references and index.
1. Self-defeating behavior.   I. Title.
BF637.S37 W35   2001
158.1—dc21

00-068082

ISBN: 978-1-58270-410-4

The corporate mission of Beyond Words Publishing, Inc.: *Inspire to Integrity*

Contents

Preface

"Why did I say that?" "I can't believe I ate all that!" "What was I thinking?" We've all asked these questions of ourselves at one time or another. Every one of us has said or done something that we later regret, even though we know better. And we're likely to do it over and over again.

As a clinical psychologist working with individuals, couples, and families for over twenty-seven years, I have met thousands of people who struggle with self-defeating patterns of thinking, feeling, and behaving. Most of them would not be considered "mentally ill." They are probably just like you. They have jobs and pay taxes; some are married and some are not. Most of them are intelligent and are motivated to change. They have control over many facets of their lives, but they can't seem to control them*selves*. They lash out at others; or they fall into addictive patterns of eating, drinking, or smoking; or they get involved in affairs; or they end up in other self-defeating cycles.

While talking through their problems is helpful, my clients also benefit from homework tasks and reading assignments. Not only do these adjuncts to psychotherapy reinforce what has been discussed in therapy sessions, but they also help people gain deeper understanding into their minds and experience what it's like to take charge of their own lives. When people truly comprehend how they came to be mired in personal problems, they can focus their energies on finding solutions. When they acquire new insights and tools for one set of problems, they can often apply these strategies to future situations.

One tool that I have found useful with my clients is the concept of the "inner brat." Not a formal psychiatric diagnosis, this inner brat is nevertheless responsible for getting us into trouble with ourselves and others. I began using the concept of the inner brat a few years ago as a way of helping people get a handle on some of their counterproductive thoughts and behaviors. At first my clients reacted with amusement, but when they saw how the idea of an inner brat could quickly bring their problems into focus, they made impressive gains in changing their self-defeating patterns. Thus came the idea for this book. If getting familiar with one's inner brat could help my clients, I reasoned, it could probably help many other people. It is not necessary to be in psychotherapy in order to benefit from the ideas and advice presented here.

If you find yourself frequently doing and saying things you later regret, you will benefit from the information and advice in this book. Chapters 1 and 2 introduce the inner brat and the many ways in which it affects your life. Chapters 3 and 4 provide brief descriptions of the general workings of the mind as well as how contemporary culture has encouraged "bratty" behavior. Chapters 5 and 6 describe the major components of the inner brat: impulsiveness and narcissism. Chapter 7 is a short quiz to help you estimate your own inner brat's dominance. Chapters 8, 9, and 10 illustrate the various mental techniques that the inner brat uses. Chapter 11 shows you how to minimize the chances that your inner brat will gain control. But if it does gain control, chapter 12 outlines specific techniques to tame it. Chapter 13 addresses specific problems in the context of the inner brat and offers suggestions for change, and chapter 14 suggests what to do about the inner brats of other people in your life.

Throughout this book are case examples. For reasons of confidentiality, these examples do not reflect the circumstances of specific people whom I have helped. They are, however, typical of many people with whom I have worked.

It is not easy to change long-standing patterns of self-defeating thoughts, feelings, and behaviors. However, it is certainly possible to do so, especially when you gain a new perspective and the right tools. This book will give you a greater understanding of why you do what you do. It will also show you how to make changes that last. If you're up to the challenge, you have a good chance of taming your inner brat once and for all.

Acknowledgments

I would like to thank Cynthia Black, publisher, for her enthusiasm and leadership in bringing this book to publication. Her editorial staff, including Julie Steigerwaldt, Carol Franks, and Marvin Moore, made helpful suggestions and asked provoking questions, which forced me to think and express my ideas with greater precision.

My esteemed colleagues, Roy Baumeister, Ph.D.; Albert Ellis, Ph.D.; Stephen Ragusea, Ph.D.; Myrna Shure, Ph.D.; and Edward Zuckerman, Ph.D., took time from their already full schedules to review the manuscript. Their insights and comments are much appreciated.

Thanks also to my husband, Tom, and my daughters Janis and Denise. They read through several first drafts, with hardly any complaining, and gave their two cents—and sometimes four cents—worth.

My office assistants, Ronda Engle and Esme Goodsir, took care of administrative tasks with their usual proficiency so that I could focus on my writing.

Kevin Lang of Bedford Bookworks saw potential in the title and encouraged me to develop my ideas. Paulette Lee helped set the search for a publisher on a firm footing.

Finally, I would like to thank the clients with whom I have worked over the years. They have taught me much about the strength of the human spirit and its ability to triumph over the most tenacious of inner brats.

1

An Inner Brat?!! Who, Me??

Deep within the recesses of our psyches there resides a brat. We each have a brat inside of us, a remnant of our childhood. This brat is responsible for much of what we hate most about ourselves. Let me explain...

While most of us would like to think of ourselves as rational beings who behave logically and have control over our emotions, this is not always the case. We do sometimes lose our tempers, give in to temptation, or say things we later regret. At such times we tend to blame other people or situations. For example, we convince ourselves that we got angry because someone provoked us, or that we just couldn't resist the delicious-looking dessert that was calling our name, or that we couldn't start working on the income-tax return because the kids were too noisy or because we had a head cold.

If these sound like excuses to you, they are. Think how dejected you'd feel if every time you didn't live up to your ideal performance you blamed your weak will, your selfish streak, or your short temper. It's much easier to think of reasons outside of yourself to account for your decisions and behavior, even when the reasons don't fully make sense. After all, you've been provoked countless times before and did not lose your temper. You've resisted dozens of delicious desserts in the past without a twinge of regret. And when April 14 rolled around, you got to the taxes—noisy children, stuffy head cold, and all.

No, it's not the situation or another person that makes you say or do things that you later regret. It's a much stronger force, a force so compelling that it seems to have a life of its own. When this force is in control, you might even feel that you're not your "normal" self. It's not the "real" you who loses your temper or succumbs to temptation or laziness. It's something inside you, but not *the* you.

This inner force acts like an immature, spoiled child who demands immediate attention and satisfaction—a brat. A brat wants what it wants, when it wants it, and doesn't care who or what is hurt or destroyed in the process. A brat also relentlessly refuses to do what it doesn't want, regardless of the consequences. All a brat cares about is itself and taking care of its own immediate needs as quickly and completely as possible.

If you find yourself acting like a brat more often than you'd care to admit, you're not alone. All of us—even the most educated, wise, and reasonable people—behave in bratty ways. You've seen bratty behavior in your parents, in your bosses, and even in your sports heroes and community leaders once in a while. Some people are aware of such behavior within themselves, but many are not. In the next few pages, you'll first meet Emily and then Dave, two people who know they behave irrationally but can't seem to stop. (All names used in this book are ficti-tious, but the situations represent those experienced by real people.)

Emily

Emily arrived at my office distraught. It had happened again. Her husband had forgotten to phone to tell her he was going to be late. By the time he came home, she was in such a rage that she called him every name in the book and threatened him with divorce.

It was her sixth psychotherapy visit. By this point, she had learned how her childhood had shaped her view of the world. Her mother's volatile temper was something that she remembered all too well, and she recalled having vowed to herself that she would never behave the way her mother had. Nevertheless, here she was, yelling at her husband and chil-dren over minor issues, only to regret it later. Moreover, just like her mother, she could not bring herself to apologize after losing her temper. Emily said, "I know I should count to ten when I get angry, or sometimes even a hundred, but something happens inside me. It's like an overpower-ing urge to hurt the person I'm mad at. I know what I *should* do and say, but for some reason, I can't control myself. I must be crazy or something."

Emily isn't crazy. She is a well-respected professional in the community with considerable experience in helping others. People come to *her* for advice. "If they only knew..." she mused. The majority of the time Emily is reasonable and approachable. But occasionally, when her emotional "hot but-tons" get pushed, she seems to turn into an angry five-year-old, complete with foot stamping, name calling, and irrational screaming. Unfortunately, these episodes are taken out on the people she cares about most—her family.

Emotional Hot Buttons

Emotional hot buttons are memories of past hurtful events or situations that once caused us anger, fear, or shame. Each of us has our own hot buttons. For some people, they may include angry voices; for others, they may encompass experiences of loss, or abandonment, or humiliation. Everyone's experience of a hot button is unique to that individual's memories, background, and personality. Emily's hot buttons are related to feelings of rejection that she experienced as a child. Her mother, a woman with a fiery temper, was quick to criticize her, even for minor mistakes. While growing up, Emily learned that if she took the initiative to dust and vacuum and wash the dishes, her mother might overlook the fact that her shoes weren't polished to a shine. She believed that if she pleased her mother often enough, her mother might someday give her a hug for no reason, just because she loved her. It is no surprise that Emily grew into a perfectionistic person herself, ever alert to signs of approval and disapproval from others. Now, whenever she feels overworked and unappreciated, she reacts as if the world has conspired against her.

A common hot button for many people is related to angry voices. If you grew up in a family where there was a great deal of fighting or physical abuse, you were probably terrified by loud voices as a child. After all, at seven or eight years old, a child has virtually no power to make the yelling stop. The memories of the loud voices stay with you forever. Years later, when a boss, a spouse, or other important person in your life raises his or her voice, you might react with anxiety or anger at a level that is out of proportion to the current situation. This reaction occurs because situations today trigger feelings that were established in the past.

Another common hot button is associated with abandonment. Most young children have been lost or separated from their parents on at least one occasion, and usually more. Since children have active imaginations, it isn't unusual for them to worry that their parents have abandoned them and won't come back. This theme is so universal that it is found in several myths and fairy tales, the most familiar of which is "Hansel and Gretel." In adulthood, the theme of abandonment takes on a symbolic as well as a literal meaning. Not only might a person be overly sensitive to a friend or lover being physically absent but also to behaviors that might *represent* emotional abandonment. If you are extremely hurt when someone is not attentive enough, when someone disagrees with you, or when someone fails to buy you the perfect gift, you are probably interpreting such actions as indicators of abandonment or desertion.

A third common emotional hot button is associated with feelings of shame and humiliation. We have all felt shame in our lives, usually triggered by our parents' admonition or public embarrassment. Shame made us feel not only powerless but also inadequate and unlovable. If you find yourself easily embarrassed by friendly teasing, if you take extra care to be more private about yourself than most people are, it is possible that one of your hot buttons is related to shaming experiences which you had as a child.

There are many different hot buttons, and they are experienced by each of us in our own unique way. How we experience these hot buttons is based on the situations we were exposed to as young children and, more importantly, how we interpreted these situations. Thus, two children in a family may have overheard the same fights between their parents, but one child may grow up to actively ignore loud voices, while the other child grows up to anticipate and overreact to them.

We all have emotional hot buttons, and most of the time they are not a problem. As we go about our daily business, we don't usually dwell on painful memories of childhood. Every now and then, however, someone will say or do something that reminds us of an intensely emotional situation from our past. *Boom!* This immediately triggers feelings similar to those we felt in the original situation. It usually happens so fast that most of us are unaware of the connection between current feelings and past events.

When our hot buttons are triggered, we react intensely—either with strong feelings, such as anger or rage, or else with behavior involving indulgent self-gratification. For example, some people fly off the handle at the first sign of frustration, while others turn to cigarettes, alcohol, or food. Such self-indulgence is viewed by many mental-health experts as an escape from certain unacceptable feelings. In any case, whether we take out our feelings on someone else or through self-indulgence, it serves as a means of immediate relief from internal discomfort. Just as infants and young children can't stand being hungry, cold, wet, or ignored, we as adults often act as if we can't tolerate the hot-button emotions that are triggered within us.

We are particularly vulnerable to having our emotional hot buttons triggered when we feel overly stressed or frustrated. At such times, it doesn't take much to send us over the edge. For example, while Emily was giving her toddler, Jeremy, a bath, she was also thinking about putting some cupcakes in the oven for her older son's school party the next day and cleaning up the kitchen. Then she reminded herself that she had to finish a report for work the next day. "How am I going to get all that done and still get to bed before midnight?" she asked herself desperately. Just then, Jeremy threw his rubber duckie into the air, and as it fell back into the water, it made a big splash all over her and the floor. Jeremy screeched in delight, but to Emily this only meant more work piled onto what she had already envisioned for the night. Without thinking, Emily yelled at Jeremy for making such a mess, and she roughly removed him from the tub.

If Emily had taken a moment to assess the situation logically, she might have responded quite differently, enjoying her son's delight. But she was already feeling stressed, and she was so self-absorbed with her own problems that she couldn't see beyond them.

Emily's reaction was purely emotional and impulsive. We would call her behavior *irrational*, that is, behavior not based on logic or reason. Given enough stress and frustration, most people behave irrationally. Instead of discussing an issue, we yell and interrupt. Rather than listening to what the other person has to say, we resort to blaming and name-calling. Such behavior is usually very self-centered and is more typical of a young child than of a mature adult.

Everyone behaves this way sometimes, even the most reasonable and mature among us. That's because the irrational force is very powerful. It stems from primitive instincts and emotions that we were all born with. This force demands immediate attention, immediate relief from discomfort, or immediate gratification. It is what I call the *inner brat*.

Social scientists and the medical profession have come up with complex-sounding names for people's tendency to give in to the impulse of the moment: low frustration tolerance, weak ego controls, difficulties with delay of gratification, superego lacunae, and a host of others. While such labels may be helpful in making specific diagnoses, they don't mean much to the average person. On the other hand, most of us have a pretty good idea of what a brat is. A brat—usually a young child—wants what it wants, when it wants it. A brat won't take no for an answer. If a brat doesn't get its way, it hollers, pouts, or carries on until someone gives in. There is no need for psychiatric jargon when we have a perfectly suitable common term to describe our self-centered, demanding impulses. (Throughout this book, the term *brat* will be referred to as of neuter gender.)

Dave

The inner brat is responsible for many addictive behaviors. Consider the case of Dave, a thirty-four-year-old computer programmer who prides himself on being rational and logical. At work, he is known for his patience in anticipating and solving computer problems. But in his personal life, he can't seem to find a solution for his addiction to tobacco. Back in college, Dave started smoking cigarettes while unwinding from studying. He figured this would be only temporary, just until he got his degree. Like most young people, he felt confident that he could quit smoking as soon as he got into the "serious" world of work. And, unfortunately, like most people who begin smoking, he found that the habit was much harder to break than he expected. For the past few months, Dave has made several attempts to quit smoking. He tried behavior therapy, nicotine gum, nicotine patches, and even an antidepressant drug approved for this purpose. Nothing helped. Dave describes it this way: "I don't know what it is that drives me to light up that cigarette. I'm a sensible person. I want to stop smoking. I can think of ten thousand reasons to quit and no logical reason to continue smoking. But then I start thinking about a cigarette, and the thought becomes stronger and stronger. Pretty soon I can't think of anything else. I *must* have that cigarette; I can't concentrate on anything else until I grab a smoke and get it over with."

Dave has come face to face with his inner brat. The inner brat seizes his attention and won't let go until it's satisfied. It reminds him just how much he *needs* that cigarette and that there is nothing more important than satisfying the urge *right now*! Dave feels at a loss about how to deal with this urge. In the presence of his craving, all logic seems to fly out the window.

We can all sympathize with Dave. If it's not cigarettes we crave, perhaps it's alcohol or chocolate. Some of us are also drawn into activities that we know are not good for us, such as overeating, gambling, excessive shopping, or spending too much time on the Internet. Each time we do something we know is bad for us, our inner brat is at work. It urges us, "Go ahead and have that ice cream. It's a hot day. You deserve a treat." It says to us, "Just one more drink, and that'll be it for the night." It alerts us, "Today is the last day of the shoe sale. You have tons of shoes at home, but these are special. You'd better grab several pair before someone else gets to them first."

Destructive Impact of the Inner Brat

The inner brat can be quite destructive. When Emily loses her temper, her husband and children remember her piercing voice and nasty words long after she has calmed down and forgotten the incident. Every time Dave gives in to his urge for a cigarette, he feels ashamed and weak. Mature adults hate to think of themselves as not having self-control. Whenever the inner brat is in charge, we are at the mercy of raw emotional impulses that can have serious consequences for ourselves and for the people around us.

In this book, you will learn more about this force inside you called the inner brat. You will learn how to recognize it and how to minimize its impact. You will also realize that even if you had an unhappy childhood, even if you didn't have the same opportunities as your peers, even if you're not as smart or good-looking as other people you know, you can still overcome self-destructive habits and behaviors.

Where Does the Brat Come From?

Of course, there is no actual brat inside our heads. The term *inner brat* is just a convenient way of describing a set of thoughts, feelings, and behaviors that originated from feelings and behaviors which we experienced and expressed as infants and young children. All young children behave in a demanding, unreasonable way at times. The "brats" are those who behave this way frequently. True brats are not born; they are created. Their parents make the common mistake of surrendering to the brat's demands just to get some peace and quiet. You've probably seen such children with their parents in the aisles of the grocery store. They are the ones who whine or argue about wanting certain kinds of cereal or cookies. First, the parents say no, but when the children start protesting loudly, the parents give in, just to keep them quiet. At home, these same children challenge their parents when it comes to following rules, bedtime routines, and accepting the word "no." If the parents are not consistent in enforcing rules and consequences, the children learn that by protesting visibly enough and for long enough, they will get what they want. Thus the cycle begins. By the time the parents realize that by giving in to their children's demands they have actually rewarded them for whining, sulking, or screaming, it's almost too much effort to turn back.

Not every child turns out to be a brat. If parents resist giving in to their children's every demand, youngsters eventually learn to wait their turn, to put work before play, and to control their anger. This takes several years, and of course, it doesn't work in every situation. As children grow toward adulthood, they are expected to exercise more and more self-control. The marks of maturity are staying cool at times of stress, knowing when to be generous and when to take care of oneself, and knowing how to make up for transgressions.

Nevertheless, no matter how mature we become, there are still remnants of old primitive emotions and impulsive reactions. Back in the recesses of our memories are the times from our infancy and early childhood when we did immediately get what we wanted, usually by screaming or whining. When these memories are triggered, none of us is so cool or so mature that we don't overreact. Periodically, we all feel that familiar, overwhelming sense of urgency about something trivial.

The part of ourselves that never matured is another aspect of what I call the inner brat. This inner brat can focus on only one thing at a time. And when it focuses, it can be relentless. Just like a spoiled child, it distracts us, pesters us, and tries to do whatever it takes to get what it wants. It doesn't like to wait, either. The longer it waits, the longer and more intensely we have to "pay." When we finally do give in to our inner brat, we have unwittingly increased the likelihood that this inner brat will try the same tactics next time, only more intensely in order to get our attention sooner.

Remember Emily, the woman who took out her anger on her family? Her inner brat had no patience. It convinced her that her husband's failure to call was a deliberate act of disrespect that must be avenged and that her young son's splashing in the tub was intended only to create more work for her.

Consider the example of Dave, the self-proclaimed reasonable man who could not resist cigarettes. His inner brat kept him focused on thinking about smoking, on the momentary relief from tension that smoking could bring. He ultimately gave in to his brat because the tension of ignoring it was too overwhelming. It was so much easier just to have the stupid cigarette and get it over with, so he could continue on with his day.

To summarize thus far, the inner brat is a part of us that never matured. It's a remnant of our early childhood that will always be with us. When our emotional hot buttons are triggered, it reacts impulsively and intensely with the goal of immediate satisfaction of its own needs. In its wake, it can leave chaos or destruction for ourselves and those around us.

What Good Does It Do to Picture Yourself as Having an Inner Brat?

Picturing an inner brat serves several important functions: It helps add objectivity, preserve self-esteem, and cut problems down to size, and it is an effective shortcut for dealing with certain problems. Research has shown that when you have some distance or objectivity, you are more effective in dealing with problems. It is for this reason that doctors are strongly advised against treating their own family members, and attorneys are reminded that "a lawyer who represents himself has a fool for a client." From your personal experience, you probably know that it's easier to see flaws in other people than in yourself. When you visualize your undesirable characteristics as belonging to an entity such as your inner brat, you gain some perspective to help you see things more clearly. At the same time, you still own responsibility for the problem. By labeling your thoughts or behaviors as a product of your own inner brat, you don't have to blame anyone else.

A second advantage to using the inner-brat notion is that it preserves your self-esteem. When you use the idea of an inner brat to reflect some of your least-liked qualities, you can see them as separate from the *real* you. Thus, you can still view yourself as a reasonable or as a basically *kind* person, albeit with a pesky brat that sometimes interferes. Considering problematic thoughts, feelings, or behaviors as belonging to such a pesky brat cuts the problems down to size. It is easier to figure out what to do about a brat than to feel at the mercy of powerful, unknown internal forces.

Finally, using the idea of an inner brat is an efficient shortcut for defining your problem, deciding what to do about it, and acting on that decision. When you use the idea of an inner brat to describe what you don't like about yourself, you immediately bring into focus the essence of how you sabotage your best intentions. There is no need for in-depth analysis of what you're thinking or feeling; you know instantly what you mean when you call parts of yourself "bratty."

The Inner Brat versus the Inner Child

Over ten years ago, several books were written about our "inner child." John Bradshaw (1990), Charles Whitfield (1987), Alice Miller (1983), and other professionals used this term to describe our childlike, creative, spontaneous "true self." This true self supposedly becomes suppressed and buried when our parents abuse us or fail to properly nurture us. In its place emerges a "wounded self," which is the source of all our emotional pain, relationship problems, and addictions. Earlier in this chapter, in the section on hot buttons, I described a few scenarios in which people can develop feelings of fear, abandonment, shame, and humiliation. Such experiences are active fodder for the proponents of the inner child, who examine them in exquisite detail.

The main task of "inner child work" is to recognize all the pain inflicted by our parents and other caregivers and to grieve over it. Through this grief process, we are urged to reexperience the anger, loneliness, sadness, and other intense emotions that we supposedly suppressed as children. Much of the inner child work is done in a group situation, which typically becomes very emotional, with much weeping, hugging, and comforting. People usually take turns giving testimony to the wounds and indignities that they suffered at the hands of their caregivers. Rage against one's parents is not only accepted, it's encouraged. While raging against parents, group participants receive affirmation that they themselves are lovable individuals, regardless of how much they've screwed up in life. Now, I am not opposed to people learning to love themselves, but to assume that the majority of their unacceptable feelings and actions were caused by their parents only renders them more

14

Stefan

helpless and self-righteous in absolving themselves of responsibility for their actions.

The ultimate goal of inner child work is to uncover one's creative, spontaneous self and to free oneself from thoughts and behaviors that interfere with harmonious relationships. However, many people stay stuck in the grieving process. Considering the focus of inner child therapy, this result is not surprising. When the initial thrust of the therapy is to uncover and examine rage and other strongly negative feelings, it is very difficult to get beyond the grief. Furthermore, the group process and well-meaning therapists legitimize such feelings as valid and necessary. Consequently, many people spend months, and even years, dwelling on the bad breaks they got as children. In their search for self-esteem, these people may never emerge from feeling victimized. ! ! !

As Don Henley wrote in a popular song in 1994, "Get over it." Everyone has experienced pain as a child. It may be true that your father beat your mother, or perhaps he even beat you. But that does not necessarily explain why you continue to drink too much, eat too much, lose your temper, or engage in other destructive behaviors. It doesn't explain why you continue to feel sorry for yourself today. What perpetuates such behaviors and thoughts is the fact that you allow yourself to continue them. Behavioral scientists have demonstrated that it isn't always necessary to have full knowledge of the origin of moods and bad habits in order to change them. Knowledge helps you understand your problem in a larger context, but insight alone is rarely sufficient to make changes. People who seek to discover their inner child typically end up with more excuses than solutions for their problems.

As you can see, the inner brat is quite different from the inner child. It is just as "real" in our personal history as is our spontaneous, creative self. Like the inner child, the inner brat developed from real experiences and real responses from our caregivers. But the inner brat is not something that we seek to nurture. Although it is important to know our inner brat, the ultimate goal is to move our inner brat from a state of prominence in our lives to a place in the background in order to minimize its interference. The inner-child approach dwells on our emotional hot buttons and their origins. It magnifies the impact of negative experiences, making us feel almost helpless to do anything about them. On the other hand, the inner brat, in part, represents the way in which we react when our emotional hot buttons are triggered. And that is something over which we *do* have control.

The Inner Child versus the Beast

The idea of a primitive "Beast" in our minds was developed by Jack Trimpey. A former alcoholic, he is very much opposed to the views of Alcoholics Anonymous, which depict the addict as a powerless victim of a disease. Trimpey established an approach called *Rational Recovery* as an alternative to Alcoholics Anonymous. In his lectures and books (the latest of which is *Rational Recovery: The New Cure for Substance Addiction*[1]), Trimpey asserts that the disease concept of addiction only serves to perpetuate blaming something other than oneself for becoming addicted. He introduced the concepts of the Addictive Voice and the Beast to show us how we give in to biological urges that "speak" to us in sinister tones. According to this approach, people are rational beings who can override biological urges through sheer force of will and determination. Rational

Recovery is gaining increasing acceptance in the field of addictions because it works by empowering people rather than telling them they are forever victims of a disease.

The inner brat is similar to Trimpey's "Beast," but I will later point out specific differences. Both the Beast and the inner brat are a convenient way of giving form to our darker side, but Trimpey's Beast is portrayed as evil, while the inner brat is mainly immature. It need not be destroyed but merely tamed.

Other Views of Childhood Influences

The notion that we are influenced by childhood memories, thoughts, and behaviors is not new. For centuries philosophers, poets, and novelists have noted similarities between people's adult personalities and their childhood temperaments. In the 1920s, Sigmund Freud was the first to propose a theory of unconscious motivation in which he claimed that forgotten experiences from childhood influence people's perceptions and decisions. Carl Jung, a contemporary of Freud, found evidence that certain ways of thinking and reacting may be inherited from past generations.

The idea that our personalities consist of more than one set of thoughts and feelings has also been explored in depth. Books such as the best-seller *I'm O.K., You're O.K.* by Thomas Harris (1973) are based on the principles of Transactional Analysis, founded by Eric Berne. This theory proposes that we all have three *ego states* which Berne calls the Parent, the Adult, and the Child. These represent various roles that we assume when interacting with other people. The ego states are derived from our own experiences and observations.

The term *inner brat,* as used in this book, is not connected in any way with the inner child as discussed by professionals in the field of chemical dependency and addiction. It is somewhat similar to the Child ego state presented by Berne, and it bears some resemblance to the unconscious motivations described by Freud and the Beast described by Trimpey.

Some of the ideas and methods in this book derive from ideas of Freud, Jung, Berne, and others. They are presented in more detail in chapter 4.

Personal Responsibility

Earlier in this chapter, I remarked that parents can create brats through overindulgence. However, they are not entirely responsible for our inner brats. We create and nurture our own inner brats by the very methods with which some parents unwittingly encourage their children to become selfish and unruly. By indulging our own inner brats over a period of years, we support them and help them grow and gain power over us.

Even if your inner brat seems to have taken over your life, there is hope. After all, it is your own brain that decides what comes out of your mouth and what you do with your limbs. Just because your inner brat is demanding attention doesn't mean that you can't resist it. In this book, you will learn several techniques for taming your inner brat. It may take some time and practice, but you are stronger than your inner brat.

In the next chapter, you will become more acquainted with the everyday impact of the inner brat. Our bratty behavior is not caused by outside forces. The inner brat is there within us, waiting for the opportunity to express itself. However, if we get to know our inner brat, we can tame it and, thereby, gain a greater sense of control over our lives.

2

The Inner Brat in Action

Always in the back of our minds, ready to satisfy its wants and desires, the inner brat lies in wait. Whenever we're faced with a frustrating situation or a challenge to our willpower, the inner brat will use a variety of tactics and manipulations to get immediate satisfaction. It is responsible for much of what we hate about ourselves. Too often the inner brat influences us to say or do things that we later regret, just because it can't tolerate even mild frustration. Representing primitive desires and impulses, the inner brat wants what it wants, when it wants it, without considering the consequences.

The inner brat operates in three main spheres: thoughts, feelings, and behaviors. In our thoughts, it talks to us, sometimes in gentle persuasive tones, sometimes in demanding, urgent tones, and sometimes in a threatening voice. Although we don't generally hear an actual voice, we do perceive thoughts running through our minds. When we find ourselves justifying our behavior or emotions, that's the inner brat trying to convince us that we are right, even though our better judgment knows otherwise.

When we grumble to ourselves or dwell on the unfairness of a situation, it is our inner brat that keeps us focused on our misery.

Most inner-brat thoughts are accompanied by unpleasant feelings. Usually these are experienced as irritability or a sense of urgency. We experience such feelings not only in our minds but also in our bodies. Every emotion has a physical sensation associated with it, but not everyone experiences the same type of physical reaction. For example, some people feel their hearts beating faster. Others sense a tightening in their throat, chest, or stomach. Still others feel weakness or tension in the muscles of the arms or legs. Just as emotional hot buttons vary from one person to the next, so do physical components of emotions.

Physical sensations are not limited to emotions connected with the inner brat. They occur with all sorts of feelings, such as when a person is excited, or frightened, or overjoyed. They can also develop in response to medications or as a result of a medical condition. These reactions are what we call *nonspecific*. That is, they occur in many different kinds of circumstances and are not necessarily diagnostic of anything in particular. They simply reflect a state of physical or emotional arousal. The body becomes aroused by any strong stimulus that is either physical (e.g., a sharp pain) or emotional (e.g., anger). Since the inner brat includes some emotional reactions, these, too, are accompanied by physical sensations.

Besides showing up in our thoughts and feelings, the inner brat also operates in our behavior. It reveals itself when we engage in activities that we know are harmful to ourselves, such as smoking, drinking, drug use, and gambling. It is implicated in overeating, in spending money we don't have, as well as in procrastinating and making excuses. The inner brat is also evident in behavior that is hurtful to other people, such as temper tantrums, sulking, and sarcasm. Many extramarital affairs involve the inner brat. The parties involved usually anticipate that their own spouses will likely be hurt, but they rationalize their circumstances in order to satisfy their own desires. Whenever we engage in behavior that we don't like to see in other people, it is probably because we gave in to our inner brat.

In this chapter, you'll be introduced to a few people who allowed their inner brats to take charge. The people's names and specific circumstances have been altered to protect their anonymity, but the basic problems described are real.

Bratty Thoughts

For the past week and a half, Neil has been dwelling on his predicament. He had thought for sure that when the boss asked for a summary of his work from last year, he would be promoted to vice president. Excited by the prospect, Neil shared the anticipated good news with his family and friends. Then came the blow: he learned that he had lost out to Maggie, a manager from another department. Although he didn't know much about Maggie's qualifications, Neil felt certain that she was promoted because of her gender. "It's not fair," he muttered to himself. "I've been working my tail off, and what do I have to show for it? Maggie just sails in here and kisses up to the president, and in no time she's up there in the inner circle. And now I have to tell everyone that I'm a failure. What's the point of trying anymore?"

Neil is bitter. With the help of his inner brat, he goes over all the reasons that his bitterness is justified. The more he dwells on this, the more he becomes convinced that the whole promotion deal was orchestrated to humiliate him. Neil's inner brat does not want him to consider logical reasons why Maggie was awarded the promotion: she had been with the company (at a different office location) three years longer and had headed up a department of twice as many people. Furthermore, she had opened up a new line of business for the company. Neil's inner brat didn't want to consider this. All it knew was that Neil and the president had played golf together and their wives were good friends. That was enough to make the inner brat dwell on the unfairness of it all.

On the other side of town, Jenny's thoughts were being influenced by her inner brat. At sixteen, she was not the most popular girl in her class, but she got good grades and had many friends—or so she thought. One day at lunch she overheard a group of girls talking about a party that they had attended the previous weekend. Apparently, many of the people she knew had been there, but she had not been invited. As she approached the group, everyone suddenly stopped talking. A couple of the girls smiled vacantly in her direction. Jenny didn't know whether to greet them or walk away. Just then the bell rang, signaling the end of lunch, and the group of girls quickly dispersed, avoiding eye contact with Jenny. Jenny felt numb. She walked to her locker, grabbed her books for the afternoon, and somehow found her way to class. All through history and biology that afternoon, she could think of nothing but that party. Her inner brat kept her focused on how much everyone must hate her. It convinced her that she must be a real loser to be excluded from that social event. She found herself plotting revenge on those girls who had betrayed her by not mentioning the party beforehand.

Jenny's inner brat could not get over the fact that she had been excluded from the party. It zeroed in on this single detail as proof that other people didn't like her. Soon it persuaded her that even those people who seemed to like her were only pretending to do so because they felt sorry for her. Had Jenny not paid attention to her inner brat, she would not have dwelled on her shortcomings, and she would not have felt the need to lash out at those whom she now perceived as her enemies.

The inner brat gets jealous, resentful, and angry. When it doesn't like what's happening, it starts mumbling, grumbling, or even yelling inside your mind. When you find yourself going over and over something that seems unfair or hard to deal with, your inner brat is engaging in an extended monologue. The longer you allow it to dwell on whatever predicament you're faced with, the more you'll end up feeling angry, resentful, or sorry for yourself.

Bratty Feelings

Bratty feelings are closely related to bratty thoughts. They affect one another. For example, when Neil didn't get the promotion, he not only dwelled on his perception of the facts of the situation, but he also felt jealous and humiliated. These feelings, in turn, stimulated more thoughts of self-pity. The more he felt sorry for himself, the more he thought of all the reasons to justify his feelings. Similarly, when Jenny overheard the girls talking about the party and realized she hadn't been invited, she felt rejected. For the rest of the afternoon her inner brat reminded her of several reasons why she was rejected. Planning her revenge on the girls was her inner brat's way of evening the score.

Inner-brat feelings include anger, jealousy, envy, and self-pity. While the latter three are directed inward, inner-brat anger is typically directed outward, often at other people. All these feelings have destructive effects, not only because of the feelings themselves but because of the thoughts and actions that they generate. When the inner brat is steeped in being angry or upset in some way, it keeps us focused on the negative. If we allow inner-brat thoughts to control us too often or for too long, not only will we develop an attitude problem, but our health may also be affected. Prolonged negative thoughts and attitudes affect the stress hormones in the body and its ability to fight disease. Research has demonstrated a link between negative attitudes and certain illnesses as well as slowness in healing.

A cautionary note: It is important to distinguish between temporary negative moods and those that last for weeks or months. If you find yourself dwelling on the negative most of the time, this may be more than your inner brat. Chronic negative feelings are one of the signs of clinical depression. If, along with constant negative feelings, you are also tired and unmotivated, find yourself overcome by sadness for no good reason, have trouble eating or sleeping, or feel nervous much of the time, you may be suffering from depression. Also, these same symptoms can reflect certain medical conditions. In any case, if you have any of these symptoms, you should consult a medical or mental-health professional.

Bratty Behaviors
Addictive Habits

One of the most common effects of the inner brat is in behavior that we call addictions and bad habits. We saw an example of this with Dave and his smoking. His efforts to quit smoking were continually sabotaged by his inner brat, who kept Dave's mind on what he craved and convinced him that he deserved—no, *needed* to have a cigarette. His thoughts became preoccupied with finding, lighting, and smoking a cigarette, to the point where other thoughts were pushed aside. The inner brat kept talking to him, pestering him, just as a bratty child would do.

Kellie knows her inner brat too well. She is almost always on a diet. She jokes that she has lost 250 pounds, although it's the same ten pounds twenty-five times over. Starting a diet is no problem for her. In her job as a fitness trainer, it is vital that she appear healthy and trim. When the bulges in her leotard can no longer be hidden by control-top panty hose, she takes diet pills and goes all out on a starvation/exercise marathon that lasts about three weeks. While preaching the importance of healthy moderation to her clients, Kellie is privately stressing her body by drastic calorie reduction and overzealous workouts. She gets fast results but needs a lot of makeup to hide the lines of fatigue on her face. During the process of dieting, she is relentless in her self-discipline. Although her inner brat tries to remind her how good chocolate tastes, she doesn't pay attention. The diet pills relieve her of the feeling of hunger (even though they do make her more than a little edgy), and her three-hour daily exercise regimen leaves her too tired to do much else besides work and sleep.

Kellie's problem with her inner brat begins after she loses her ten pounds, stops taking the diet pills, and resumes her normal schedule. Usually after her weight loss, she makes a promise to herself not to let the pounds creep back again. She vows to eat a healthful diet, avoid junk food, and exercise in moderation, just as she recommends to her clients. But first, after those weeks of Spartan deprivation, Kellie feels entitled to a little treat. This is where her inner brat makes its appearance. It reminds her of all the calories she burned in the last couple of weeks and assures her that a few more cookies won't affect her weight. Since it takes about 3,600 excess calories to gain a pound of body weight, Kellie listens to her inner brat and agrees that she can eat several cookies without guilt. Now her inner brat has its hold on her. For the next several days, it reminds her of her recent deprivation, persuading her to eat more and more junk food. Her inner brat loves anything greasy, salty, and sweet. If all three of those qualities are in a single food, so much the better.

Eventually, Kellie notices that she's gained a couple of pounds. "Not to worry," rationalizes her inner brat, "it's just temporary water weight." But this water weight seems to hang around longer than expected. Soon Kellie's inner brat convinces her to stop weighing herself. Her ten-pound cycle is underway again.

Habits are difficult to break. Addictive habits are especially problematic, because they involve not only psychological cravings but physical symptoms as well. Anyone who has quit smoking or who has stopped excessive use of alcohol or drugs will tell you that, for the first few days, the body undergoes a period of withdrawal that may include dizziness, light-headedness, tremors, and other highly uncomfortable sensations. These are the body's reaction to an abrupt withdrawal of a substance that it has become used to.

Withdrawal has a mental or psychological component as well. Just thinking about what you're giving up can precipitate some of the same uncomfortable symptoms as those caused by actual physical withdrawal.

When your inner brat gets you obsessed with feeling deprived, your body often responds *as if* it's in need of a "fix." Thus, long after the body should have adjusted to the absence of the alcohol, tobacco, caffeine, sugar, or other substance, you may still experience episodes of light-headedness just by imagining having some again.

Jim gets his fix from alcohol. He decided long ago that he's not an alcoholic because he doesn't drink every day. He drinks only when he's had a stressful day and needs to relax. His problem is that, once he's had his first gin and tonic, he goes for five or six more. By the end of the evening, he's passed out on the couch, oblivious to everything around him.

Jim first arrived at my office with his wife, Laura, mainly because she had threatened divorce unless he went for marriage counseling. At their initial session, Laura did most of the talking. "About three or four nights a week," she began, "Jim comes home, says he's too tired to eat dinner, fixes himself a gin and tonic, and plops himself in front of the TV. The kids and I eat without him. By the time I'm done helping the kids with homework, supervising baths, and tucking them into bed, Jim's probably had several drinks. He's in no mood for conversation, so I just go upstairs and watch TV in bed by myself until I fall asleep. It hasn't been much of a marriage for several years, ever since our second child was born."

It was obvious that this relationship needed a major overhaul. Jim's drinking was only one of the problems, but it was a major obstacle to getting back on track. After a few sessions, both Jim and Laura recognized that, in her zealous attention to the children, she had little energy left for her husband. Similarly, Jim's commitment to his career overshadowed his involvement with both his wife and family. They recalled the fun and sense of camaraderie that had brought them together in the first place and promised to set aside time for each other.

While addressing these issues, Jim minimized the impact of his drinking. As long as he could blame his wife for ignoring him, he didn't need to confront the fact that, with or without her attention, he still relied too much on alcohol to calm himself. Over the past few years, alcohol had become more than a medication; it had also become a friend. This fact became obvious one Saturday night when the couple had arranged for a baby-sitter and got tickets to a play downtown. The day had not been particularly stressful. Jim had spent most of the afternoon working in the yard and cleaning the lawn mower. When he came in from outside, he automatically went to the liquor cupboard. From the next room Laura heard the sound of ice dropping into a glass, and she knew immediately that the evening was shot. Walking into the kitchen she begged, "Jim, please don't. You know what happens when you start drinking."

Jim replied, "Don't worry. I'm just going to have one drink. It was hot out in that yard." An hour and three drinks later, Jim complained of a headache and asked his wife to call the baby-sitter and cancel their date. He was too tired to go out. Laura had experienced this routine before, but it hurt especially now because they were both supposedly working on renewing their relationship.

At their next session with me, we addressed Jim's drinking directly. After thirty minutes of denying that it was a problem, he finally admitted that he didn't think he could live without alcohol. He had tried to tell himself in the past several weeks that his wife and family were more important than the booze, but there was this nagging voice in the back of his mind that kept demanding just one more gin and tonic. This voice wouldn't leave him alone. It kept reminding him that he shouldn't be controlled by anyone, including his psychologist and, especially, his wife. As the voice seductively described the sense of calm that a few sips of alcohol could bring, Jim felt shaky just thinking about it.

When I suggested to Jim that he designate that voice as his inner brat, he looked puzzled. "Think about it," I said to him. "It nags and whines and manipulates, just like some of those unruly children you see at the mall. And when you give in, it stops, at least for the moment."

Jim could see my point. He thought about that nagging voice in the back of his mind. Indeed it did remind him of a brat. I added, "You've probably learned, from experience with your own kids, that the more you give in to that kind of whining, the more likely it is that they'll resort to the same behavior next time." With this insight, Jim began to recognize his inner brat and to work on ways to control it.

The inner brat is instrumental in most addictive habits: smoking, drinking, gambling, drug use, Internet addiction, and even uncontrolled eating and shopping. It also comes into play when a person engages in marital infidelity. In each case, the inner brat demands immediate gratification, using persuasion, arguments, threats, or whatever it takes to get what it wants. Of course, all of these "conversations" that the inner brat has with you are internal, and sometimes they happen so automatically you don't even realize it. But if you stop to listen to your thoughts, you will find variations of some of the examples described thus far.

Self-Defeating Behaviors

As we've seen from examining addictive habits, your inner brat tries to get you to do something that you know is bad for you. It also sometimes tries to have you avoid doing something that you know is good for you. The most common example is procrastination. Everyone procrastinates at times, especially when the task is difficult or time-consuming. Just like a whiny child, your inner brat doesn't want to exert itself at something that requires planning or extended effort.

Every year, during the second week in April, Bill's stomach hurts. It's not from something he ate; it's from realizing that his income-tax forms are due on April 15, and he hasn't even begun to get them ready. After last year's stomachache, Bill purchased a computer program to make it simpler to fill out his tax forms, but he never got around to installing it onto his computer. He had also promised himself to start organizing his tax records by the end of January, but time had somehow got away from him. Now, with a filing deadline only days away, he is frantically trying to find his W-2 form and to locate all the other papers that he needs. It's not as if Bill hadn't thought about filing his tax return this year. In fact, he thought about it plenty. It's just that whenever he did think about it, his inner brat welled up inside him and convinced him that he had plenty of time. "Besides," the inner brat would ask seductively, "what would you rather do: look for a bunch of boring papers or watch this fascinating TV show?" Then Bill's inner brat went on to promise him that next weekend, for sure, the taxes would get done.

In contrast to Bill, Jack doesn't have a problem with doing paperwork. In fact, he loves to be busy at his desk. His inner brat appears when he thinks about physical exertion. For the past several months, Jack has made plans to start exercising more. With a history of heart disease in his family, exercise is more than a means to look better; it's vital to his health. Jack joined a health club but went only a few times. He can't recall just how he stopped going altogether, but he does remember that there were a few rainy days when it seemed too much effort to leave the apartment. Then he started bringing work home and didn't have time to exercise. Now, after having attended a former classmate's funeral, Jack is once again planning to begin an exercise routine. He doesn't realize that as long as he lets his inner brat determine whether it feels like exercising, he won't stick to his promise. Jack's inner brat uses various tactics to put off exercise. It complains that the weather's too cold or too hot, or that it's too late or too early. Then it promises it will be ready to exercise later in the week. Of course, when that time rolls around, the inner brat begins its routine all over again.

Marie has a similar procrastination problem with her inner brat. A first-year college student, she finds herself staying up all night before a test because she didn't start studying earlier. It's not that she hadn't known a test was coming up; the date was printed on the course outline she'd received on the first day of class. But somehow, other things seemed more important. The closer she got to the test date, the more she felt an urgent need to clean her dorm room, iron her clothes, and organize her dresser drawers. Her inner brat, trying to avoid the discipline of studying, convinced her that these mundane tasks could not wait.

The main emotion underlying procrastination is anxiety, a form of fear. When we're not sure if we can accomplish what we expect of ourselves, we feel unsettled and anxious. In order to reduce our anxiety, we

Anxiety = fear

typically promise ourselves that we'll get around to the task later. In other words, we procrastinate. This promise brings a sense of relief.

Procrastination is all too common, mainly because it gives people a false sense of security. Just promise yourself you'll get to your taxes or your exercise or your homework later, and you feel better immediately. The only problem is that this relief lasts only a little while—just until the next time you have to face what you didn't accomplish. People who repeatedly give in to procrastination are controlled by their inner brat. They are all too willing to let their inner brat relieve them of anxiety by rationalizing that this is the wrong time to begin the task or by promising that they'll be more motivated next week. The inner brat will do anything to avoid facing the possibility that it may not be able to accomplish what it thinks it should.

Overreactions to Angry Feelings

Problems with addictive habits and self-discipline harm primarily the person who engages in the habit or resists self-discipline. When it comes to behaviors of the inner brat that arise from feelings of anger and rage, however, the primary adverse effect is on other people.

Earlier, we met Emily, who lashed out at her husband and children over minor frustrations. The inner brat has little patience. When it encounters obstacles, it overreacts to them, sometimes with grave results.

What about the notion that it's important to express our anger so that it doesn't get "bottled up"? Isn't it harmful to hold in angry feelings because they accumulate and explode later on? To some extent, this is true, particularly when the inner brat dwells on them and obsesses about them. On the other hand, behavior that we associate with a quick temper is best held in check. Research shows that when we "blow off steam," we become more aggressive rather than less. Angry behavior amplifies the adrenaline surge through our bodies, increasing the level of hostility even more. Any parent who has spanked a child knows that, in a series of smacks, the intensity increases from the first slap to the last. Parents who abuse their children don't start out thinking, "I want to bruise or maim my child." They are usually just angry and tense and, via their inner brat, seek to relieve the tension by hitting the child. Rather than reduce tension, the hitting increases it, and the parent continues to hit harder and harder. In the process, anger has gone out of control.

The potentially harmful effects of uncontrolled anger are not limited to the home. News reports of road rage have become more and more common. Some people become so enraged behind the wheel that they use guns to shoot other drivers who get in their way or who challenge them. One can only imagine what their inner brats must be saying: "How dare he cut in front of me! He's not going to get away with this!" or "Flip me the finger, did he? Well, I'm going to show him that nobody makes a fool out of me! That driver's gonna pay!" Road rage is an extreme manifestation of the inner brat. Thankfully, most people who get this angry don't have a gun handy. Nevertheless, they can still be dangerous. An angry person drives more aggressively, increasing the likelihood of an accident.

I have worked with individuals who were referred to me for evaluation and psychotherapy by their attorney or by the court. In almost every case, their explanation for their road rage was that the other driver made them angry. Rarely did they recognize that they lacked control over their own behavior. During the course of psychotherapy, it was helpful for them to picture an inner brat as a way of giving their anger a name. Once they had this tangible label, they could better recognize early stages of rage and take charge before their inner brat did.

Tantrums and road rage are not the only forms of angry behavior displayed by the inner brat. Sulking and pouting are other expressions of anger, but presented in a more indirect manner. Sara came to see me because she had felt worthless and unhappy for a long time. As I got to know her, I learned that she had been raised by a critical mother whom she felt she could never please. Growing up, Sara had never challenged her mother, and at age twenty-nine, she still kept silent when her mother criticized her clothes, her career, and her choice of friends. She enjoyed her job as manager of a retail clothing store but dreaded visits from the district supervisor. Whenever the supervisor stopped by, the woman would find something wrong with the store. One day it was a display that was too far in the corner; another day it was lack of sales staff to greet customers. Sara didn't know how to deal with this woman. She felt unfairly criticized, particularly since the store's profits were on the increase.

There were several things that Sara could have done, including talking to the district supervisor about her approach. But having become accustomed to avoiding confrontation, Sara said nothing. It wasn't that she didn't communicate. She communicated with icy silence. When the district supervisor came to the store, Sara would answer her questions in monosyllables, avoid eye contact, and sigh loudly as the woman walked through the store. Later, she would complain to her friends about how poorly she had been treated. Meanwhile, the district supervisor reported back to her company that, although sales were good at the store, Sara's attitude was a major problem. She recommended closer observation over Sara's performance, a recommendation that, of course, intensified Sara's reactions.

Whenever Sara perceived criticism, her inner brat felt compelled to retaliate. Its style was not confrontational but, rather, *passive aggressive*. It expressed hostility in an indirect way, fuming and sulking rather than shouting, but its target (in this case, the district supervisor) got the message just the same.

As we have seen from the case examples in this chapter, the inner brat operates in our thoughts, our feelings, and our behaviors. We hear it as a voice in the back of our minds, and we feel it in our bodies. The inner brat is the basis for much of our resentment, anger, envy, jealousy, and self-pity. It is also instrumental in our actions, including in our habits, addictions, and angry outbursts. Although the inner brat can be viewed as an entity somewhat separate from our true "self," it is, at the same time, a part of us. The inner brat is simply a convenient name for describing our darker side. We still remain personally responsible for our words and actions.

The inner brat does not operate randomly. It is based on established psychological principles, which are described in chapter 4. Inner brats assume different "personalities," varying in their characteristics from one person to another. Your inner brat is different from mine. In chapters 7 and 8, you will learn how to recognize your own inner brat and the situations in which it takes control. Although you will never eliminate your inner brat, you can learn strategies to tame it. These are described in chapter 12. The forces and principles comprising the inner brat were not originally intended to do harm. To the contrary, they became established in order to protect our self-esteem. We will examine this in the next chapter.

3

Face It—It Is Your Fault

Comedian George Carlin has observed, "Have you ever noticed? Anybody going slower than you is an idiot, and anyone going faster than you is a maniac." That's why, when we are in a hurry, the leisurely driver in front of us is an "idiot" who, for all we know, may have been deliberately put on this earth to make us late. And when we are taking our time, the driver who passes us is a "maniac" who is out to destroy everything in his path. From our self-centered point of view, it is never *we* who are in the way.

We all make mistakes, some of us more than others. But except for a small minority, we tend to be more forgiving of our own mistakes than those of others. We are sometimes so self-centered that we believe the world revolves around ourselves. And if we do happen to make a mistake, such as forgetting to use a turn signal as we slow down, we don't see it as a reflection on our character. We don't usually attach the label of "idiot" or "maniac" to ourselves. Instead, we explain our actions as minor lapses that have nothing to do with our own personality. For example, we might rationalize that we were distracted by something in the situation, such as a song on the radio or an attractive pedestrian. On the other hand, if someone else forgets to use a turn signal, we are not so charitable. More likely than not, we view the other motorist as deficient in driving skills.

Such a double standard—one set of rules for ourselves and another set for other people—is quite common. As rational beings, we always look for cause and effect in the world around us. When we observe other people's behavior, we try to explain it in terms that make sense to us at the moment. But our minds also bias our perceptions such that we minimize our own shortcomings. For example, on occasion I have knocked over my drinking glass at the dinner table. When this last happened, I said to myself, "What was that glass doing there?" as if it were the glass's fault, not mine. On the other hand, years ago when my young children spilled their drinks, I would immediately react with, "Stop fooling around!" In other words, when I knocked over my own glass, I blamed it on external circumstances; when my children spilled something, I attributed it to their own carelessness. The double standard is also evident when we accidentally bump into someone. In such a situation, we usually say, "Excuse me," and move on without much thought. In contrast, when someone bumps into us, we are more apt to think (or even say), "Hey, watch where you're going!" In the next section, I'll explain why we do this.

How We View Cause and Effect of People's Actions

Psychologists who have studied the way in which we attribute cause and effect have found a pattern. Most people account for their own small mistakes in terms of temporary or accidental factors. For example, when we forget to return a phone call, we will often say to ourselves "Oops" or something similar. After all, forgetting every once in a while is only human. But when someone else does the same thing, we are more likely to attribute it to his or her own permanent shortcomings; that is, "That person is so inconsiderate." There is a reason for this discrepancy. In order to preserve our sense of importance and self-esteem, our psychological defenses try to protect us from admitting our own imperfections and irrationalities. For most of us, the more our self-esteem is threatened, the more likely we are to blame circumstances rather than ourselves.

Here is another example: Suppose you studied hard for a test and were confident going into it but ended up getting a C. Rather than attribute the mediocre grade to mediocre intelligence or poor preparation, you will probably blame the professor, the temperature of the air in the testing room, your lack of access to vital information, or some other external factor. Not everyone reacts this way, of course. There are always a few people with extremely low self-esteem who blame themselves for just about everything. Whenever anything goes wrong, they believe that it was somehow their own fault. But the majority of people skew their perceptions in a manner that is quite self-forgiving.

While we generally attribute our own mistakes and failures to situational factors, we tend to take full credit for our successes. Listen to the post-game interviews at major athletic events. The winning team members attribute their victory to a great coach, to their own team cohesiveness, to their strong determination, or to their belief in God. You never hear the coach of the winning team say, "We won because we were lucky." On the other hand, it's not unusual for the losing team to rationalize their situation by citing weather, lack of scoring opportunities, or the other team's luck.

Summarizing thus far, we tend to credit ourselves for our successes and to blame the situation for our failures. Our inner brats thrive on these tendencies to blame anything but ourselves when things go wrong and to take full credit when things go well. In this way, inner brats can justify never having to make changes or adaptations.

The process of attribution also holds true for those with whom we identify, such as family members, heroes, mentors, our home teams, and the candidates we voted for. In the impeachment hearings of President Clinton in 1999, his admirers and loyal supporters acknowledged that he was not entirely truthful in a grand jury hearing. Nevertheless, they argued, this "lack of truthfulness" did not justify the aggressive actions of the independent counsel who relentlessly pursued incriminating evidence; nor did it justify the time and energy spent by the legislature on this "minor" issue. In other words, it was the fault of other people that the president suffered legal woes and humiliation.

In my own professional work, I have met parents who attribute their children's poor achievement to substandard teaching; I have known people who were fired from jobs because of "unfair" bosses; I have listened to jilted lovers complain about how they were misunderstood. Time and time again, people minimize shortcomings in themselves and in those with whom they identify, and they blame circumstances or other people for their problems.

The way in which we make attributions about other people is the reverse of how we account for our own behavior. When it comes to explaining the actions of other people with whom we don't identify, we tend to view their successes as due to circumstances or chance and their failures as a product of their personalities. Thus, for example, when a business competitor lands a lucrative contract, we might say to ourselves, "That was easy for him; he had good family connections." Or when an athlete from another country wins an Olympic gold medal, we might attribute this to a favorable time slot in the competition or to judges' partiality to the winning athlete's country of origin. In both these cases, circumstances and luck are viewed as the main reason for other people's accomplishments.

When it comes to unfavorable outcomes for those whom we don't know or don't identify with, our first inclination is to hold the individual personally responsible. Thus, when a prominent citizen in our community gets arrested, people who don't know him are apt to assume that he must have committed the crime for which he is being accused. Or if company headquarters announce that profits were not high enough to generate across-the-board raises, many employees attribute this to the company president's poor decision-making skills.

Social psychologists have explored this phenomenon of attribution in hundreds of studies. They conclude that it's a common phenomenon, especially in Western culture. The fact that it commonly occurs does not make it desirable, however. The most destructive example of attribution occurs in our society's strained racial relations. Because of limited trust among various racial groups and because of limited contact between individuals from these groups, the attributions that we normally make are exaggerated. Black customers browsing in a department store are regarded with suspicion by white clerks. Black drivers are more likely to be stopped by police than white drivers. It is no coincidence that our jails are populated by predominantly minority races. A largely white court system is more likely to attribute criminal intent to a nonwhite citizen and to attribute mitigating circumstances to a white citizen.

For the most part, people are not even aware of the bias in their attributions. They carry on their lives, rationalizing their own mistakes as minor errors while ascribing character defects to other people who make similar blunders. Some people are more biased than others. We all know individuals—perhaps even yourself?—who take the attribution phenomenon to the extreme. They are *never* to blame for anything they said or did, and they are quick to blame others when something goes wrong.

The "Victim" Explosion

While there have always been individuals who don't accept responsibility for their actions and predicaments, the past two decades saw an explosion in the number of people and groups who viewed themselves as victims, even when they were the ones saying or doing hurtful things to other people. Rather than apologize, they blamed it on the fact that their parents were alcoholics, or that they were abused, or that they were the target of unfair treatment by others.

Victimization became so commonplace that our language began to reflect our resistance to accepting responsibility. In the 1970s, alcoholism and its damaging effects to oneself and one's family was defined as a disease—no more shameful than diabetes. As one celebrity after another announced being a victim of this disease, it became downright respectable to be an alcoholic. Betty Ford, a former first lady, founded a treatment center, which still attracts hundreds of people every year, many of whom proclaim their addiction almost as a badge of honor.

Once alcoholism was fully entrenched as a disease, the widely accepted assumption was that the "victim" had a biological predisposition to this disease, even though no one has found conclusive evidence of a specific gene or other biological marker. Furthermore, if it was a disease, one was forever "afflicted" with it and had no control over it: once an alcoholic, always an alcoholic. According to the tenets of Alcoholics Anonymous, one is never cured or "recovered" but perpetually "recovering." Since recovery is such a painful process, the status of the recovering alcoholic has been elevated to that of hero.

Other addictions followed the same path as alcoholism. Narcotics Anonymous for drug addicts became the counterpart to Alcoholics Anonymous. Gamblers Anonymous followed shortly thereafter. The latest addiction is Internet addiction, for which, ironically, help is available online.

The addiction decades of the '70s and '80s infused the English language with the ubiquitous suffix -aholic. Words like shopaholic, foodaholic, chocaholic, workaholic, and sportsaholic are familiar to all of us. The *Cambridge Dictionary* defines the suffix -aholic as "unable to stop doing or taking." Indeed, when we describe ourselves as shopaholics or workaholics, there is an implication that we are victims of uncontrollable urges.

John Leo, columnist for *U.S. News and World Report*, quoted Marion Barry, mayor of Washington, D.C., as defending his lying about being chemically dependent: "That was the disease talking. I did not purposely do that to you. I was a victim."[2] So successful was Mr. Barry in projecting an addict/hero image that he was reelected as mayor of Washington after serving prison time for cocaine possession.

In the past couple of decades, absolving oneself of responsibility was implied not only through the language of addiction but in the very way events were explained. Phrases like "mistakes were made" and "lives were lost" were used to explain a host of government blunders. Such use of the passive voice suggests that no one was personally accountable. In the courts, we witnessed a series of defendants blaming their criminal actions on their blood sugar (as in the controversial 1978 "Twinkie defense"[3]), their menstrual cycles, or their uncontrollable passions. It was as if to say, "It's my biology, your honor. I have no control over it."

In the '80s and '90s, victimhood became institutionalized. Racial and ethnic minorities, gay and lesbian groups, feminist groups, and people with various illnesses and disabilities all marched on the Capitol to proclaim that they were victims of oppression and discrimination. Government programs began to spring up to "protect" certain groups. One such program is the Americans with Disabilities Act of 1992. Originally designed to protect people from job discrimination, it has resulted in a tangled mess of litigation focused on what constitutes a disability and who is entitled to special treatment.

I'm not implying that oppression and discrimination don't exist. History demonstrates that various groups and individuals have been treated egregiously since the beginning of civilization. However, in recent years, the United States has come to endorse victimization in even the most dubious of circumstances. For example, college campuses in the '80s began a campaign of political correctness that intruded on students' private lives. Courses emphasizing women's victimization at the hands of men and policies labeling certain acts as harassment (e.g., a young man energetically pursuing a young woman) all served to justify people's perception of their own suffering. People who were offended by language, by art, and by other people's glances—and even by their perfume—reacted in a militant fashion to have the offenders removed and/or punished.

In 1991, Professor Anita Hill accused Clarence Thomas, a candidate for Supreme Court Justice, of sexual harassment, which had allegedly occurred several years previously when they had worked together. The congressional hearings surrounding this issue had major impact on our society. Legislation was passed to protect people from threats to one's employment should they refuse a supervisor's or co-worker's advances. Fortunately, many people, especially women, got the respect they deserved through these laws. At the same time, however, women who had never perceived themselves as victims in the workplace complained now of being offended by a male co-worker's swimsuit calendar, by off-color jokes, or by mere glances and body language.

Sexual-harassment lawsuits reached a peak in the late 1990s. Thankfully, they are decreasing in number, partly due to employers' sensitivity to issues of harassment. But this trend also reflects a general overcautiousness in the workplace. Nowadays, office procedure manuals contain warnings that male supervisors must not even compliment their female employees' attire, lest they be accused of victimizing women.

The National Obsession with Personal Rights and Entitlements

Around the same time that American society became preoccupied with victimhood, it also became obsessed with "rights." Animal rights, gay rights, women's rights, children's rights—these became the focus of political and economic battles. While the goals were noble and seemed egalitarian at the time, this emphasis on rights had an unexpected effect on society. People became so concerned with their own rights and entitlements that they failed to take into account other people's rights. Ethnic and special-interest groups became increasingly polarized and distrusting, dealing with one another through angry confrontation rather than through compromise and cooperation.

Nowhere is this sense of personal entitlement more clearly expressed than in the current state of the American insurance industry and the civil court system. The underlying premise of insurance is that when you suffer a loss, you will be compensated for it. Most insurance policies cover losses due to unforeseen circumstances or one's own negligence. These losses include house fires originating from careless disposal of cigarettes, accidentally driving one's car into a ditch, or losing a diamond ring. Other policies cover damages in which a person's actions result in causing harm to someone else. These are called liability policies. So, for example, if you accidentally drive your car into another car, your auto insurance (depending on the policy) will probably pay for not only the damage to your own car but also the damage to the other person's vehicle. Furthermore, if you or the other person were injured in the accident, medical bills would also be covered in the insurance settlement.

In the early days of insurance compensation, accident victims were reimbursed only for their financial losses, including medical bills, time lost from work, and property damage. But there are also intangible losses in the form of emotional distress. After an accident, it is not uncommon to experience anxiety, sleeplessness, and other emotional symptoms. The courts have recognized that such symptoms (which they call "pain and suffering") deserve additional compensation. But this is getting out of hand. In recent years increasing numbers of plaintiffs have sued for very specific and often dubious "damages" such as not being able to play tennis, not being an active sexual partner to their spouse, and general loss of enjoyment of life.

The victim mentality has generalized from accidents to illnesses, most notable lung cancer. Tobacco companies have been successfully sued by smokers who developed cancer. These lawsuits were successful partly because lower-court case proceedings revealed that certain tobacco companies added chemicals to cigarettes to make them more addictive. They also knew about the link between smoking and cancer but chose to suppress it. Nevertheless, the surgeon general's warning that smoking may be hazardous to your health has appeared on every package of cigarettes since 1965. People used tobacco knowing of this risk and then later blamed the tobacco company when they developed cancer.

Nowadays one does not even have to be physically injured in order to claim damage. In the summer of 1999, a Michigan man was charged and convicted for using foul language within earshot of women and children. People have sued their neighbors for emotional distress caused by rude language. Such suits are handled under some homeowners' insurance policies. Rather than take the case to court, where a sympathetic jury might award huge punitive damages, the insurance companies settle out of court.

A commonly accepted belief in our society is as follows: If I am inconvenienced in any way, someone must pay. Such an attitude helps explain why so many people sue others for circumstances that they bring upon themselves. Consider the 1994 jury award of $2.9 million to a woman who sued McDonald's after spilling a cup of hot coffee that she had placed between her legs, which resulted in severe skin burns. (It should be noted that she never collected this amount. The judge later reduced the amount, and McDonald's appealed. She subsequently settled for a much reduced sum.)

Not all cases are as sensational as the McDonald's one. But every day people fill our courts seeking payment after falling off a ladder, tripping on a sidewalk, or having other accidents that are not necessarily anyone's fault. And they win!

Not too long ago I saw one of my attorney friends. He was on crutches. When I asked him what had happened, he replied that he slipped on the ice while shoveling snow in front of his office. "The worst part," he said, jokingly, "is that I own the building, so there's no one I can sue."

The Self-Help Movement

Self-help books of the '80s reflected the victim mentality of the times. It was during this period that the concept of the "inner child" became prominent. Popularized by Charles Whitfield, M.D., the "inner child" was described as "the part of each of us which is ultimately alive, energetic, creative and fulfilled; it is our Real Self—who we truly are."[4] Dr. Whitfield went on to say, "When this Child Within is not nurtured or allowed freedom of expression, a false or co-dependent self emerges. We begin to live our lives from a victim stance, and experience difficulties in resolving emotional traumas."[5]

Other authors expanded on this notion. The inner child eventually came to represent our repository of past hurts and injustices. We were exhorted to find our inner child, to listen to it, to relive its pain, and to nurture it. "Inner Child" workshops sprang up all over the country, teaching people how to accomplish these tasks.

There is nothing wrong with self-reflection and understanding ourselves. But to focus on the pain and to analyze it, as if we should have somehow been immune from any hurt in our childhood, only serve to give more validity to victimhood.

"Inner Child" workshops were one of the many support groups that became popular in the '80s and '90s. Support groups were originally set up to help people who share a common problem to endure the pain and find new hope. There are many types of support groups: those for people who have lost a child; for people with a debilitating illness; for people going through life transitions such as divorce, unemployment, or widowhood. A well-run support group can make a big difference in its members' lives. For example, research shows that women with breast cancer survived longer when they joined a professionally run support group.

However, many support groups, especially those focused on victimhood, became nothing more than pity parties. They legitimized the pain to the point where that's all that was talked about during group. Everyone shared personal pain, and no one had any solutions.

In summary, the past two decades gave rise to two major societal phenomena: an elevated sense of victimhood and an inflated definition of personal rights. We evolved into a nation of whiners and complainers. We became very self-centered, preoccupied with our own sense of entitlement.

We eventually embraced the notion that we should never have to be inconvenienced, let alone suffer, and that if we were hurt or offended, someone else had to pay.

Despite all this, we have still managed to view ourselves as basically kind and compassionate. By labeling anything that upsets or disturbs us as an injustice, we can rationalize our complaining. We legitimize our anger and our self-pity. This is the perfect growing environment for the inner brat.

4

The Inner Brat and the Forces within Us

In the last chapter, we learned that most people tend to give themselves credit for anything good that happens but blame other people or circumstances when the outcome is not so favorable. We also observed how social and economic conditions have contributed to the notion that when anything unpleasant happens to us, we are poor victims who deserve compensation. The more we embrace such a notion, the more self-centered, demanding, and "bratty" we become.

This doesn't mean that we are at the mercy of social forces or that we have no choice about our perceptions and attitudes. But to some extent, we are predisposed to think, feel, and react in certain ways. Some of this is due to inborn temperament, but much of it is learned. Researchers have demonstrated that even deeply entrenched behavior can be modified, although it takes considerable effort and practice.

The inner brat constitutes a set of thoughts, feelings, and behaviors that have been with you since very early in your childhood. They didn't get there by accident; in fact, at one time they probably served a useful purpose. But these bratty thoughts, feelings, and behaviors have long outlived their usefulness. They occur more out of habit now, and their effect is an inner brat that is potentially destructive to yourself and to those around you.

A Force to Be Reckoned With

Up to this point, I've depicted the inner brat as if it's a distinct part of the brain that can be measured or viewed with modern imaging techniques. It would be nice to think of a little imp inside our heads or a little devil that sits on our shoulder—across from the angel on the other shoulder. If that were the case, all we'd have to do is send it some tranquilizing medicine. But it's not that simple.

No one has ever actually seen an inner brat, although we've all seen its effects. The term is just a convenient way of describing various ways of thinking, feeling, and behaving. It's not just one behavior or one feeling but rather a cluster. There are many different clusters that make up bratty behaviors. (Chapter 8 will describe various personalities of inner brats.)

For now, let's just assume that the inner brat is the part of us that lashes out when we feel victimized by the outside world or when we engage in behavior that is destructive or self-defeating. For example, consider Amy, a news reporter for a small-town television station. When a news anchor position opened up, the director encouraged her to interview for the job. Amy, of course, jumped at the chance, confident that she would be selected. After all, she had been with the station for almost two years and had received good feedback about her enthusiastic style of reporting. Imagine her dismay when, in the end, the station hired

Michelle, a former reporter from out of town. "That's so unfair!" Amy exclaimed. "They almost *promised* me that job." This had been her one chance for a major career move, and now it was gone, through no fault of her own. The more Amy thought about it, the more resentful she became. Her resentment showed in her work. Her characteristic enthusiasm began to fade, affecting her on-air personality. She thought to herself, "Why bother trying? I'll just do what I have to until my contract expires and look for a job with another station."

In the back of her mind, Amy realized that her anger and her antagonistic frame of mind were jeopardizing her future opportunities. If she were to change jobs now, she knew that with her current attitude problem, she could count on getting only lukewarm letters of recommendation. Furthermore, she had seen herself on tape and recognized her lack of enthusiasm. Who would want to hire such a sourpuss?

Several times a week Amy promised herself that she would try to do better. But every time she saw Michelle sitting at the anchor desk during the broadcast, Amy felt an overwhelming urge to punish the boss at the television station. Her need for revenge began to spread to Michelle, who hadn't really done anything to Amy; in fact, Michelle went out of her way to be nice to her.

Amy struggled with trying to convince herself that staying angry was going to hurt her in the long run. But she just couldn't let go of the feeling. She was engaged in mental conflict. Despite an awareness of what she was doing to herself, Amy continued along a self-destructive path, propelled by her inner brat. It would not back down, even though she tried to push it out of her mind.

Mental Conflict

Like Amy, we all have moments when we know logically that we're being unreasonable or self-destructive but continue doing it anyway. We are also faced with mental conflict in decisions every day, although not all of them are potentially destructive. When you get dressed in the morning, should you wear the blue shirt or the beige one? Should you have toast or cereal for breakfast? Which task will you take on first at work? Such decisions have pros and cons on both sides. They do entail some degree of conflict, but usually the results are inconsequential.

Then there are moral decisions. Suppose you get too much change from the vending machine. Would you report it? Most people would not, even though they know the extra money does not belong to them. If your friend asks your opinion about her new outfit, what would you say if you don't find it particularly flattering on her? You were taught that "honesty is the best policy," but you make exceptions. How do you decide what those exceptions are?

We're familiar with rules of conduct, but we also use judgment to decide how precisely we heed them. People vary in how strongly they conform to rules and customs. Some rigidly adhere to everything that is a law or an ethical edict. These are the people who never drive above the speed limit, who never tell white lies, and who are never late in paying bills. They are punctual to a fault and usually maintain a firm schedule. These people feel secure in knowing that they always do the right thing. At the other extreme are individuals who refuse to conform unless faced by threat of punishment. They will lie in order to win an advantage; they ignore schedules and don't care if they're late. Their manner of dress and their conduct announce to the world that they are their own masters.

The rigid conformists and the defiant nonconformists have a single standard to which they adhere or against which they rebel. They don't have to make many decisions, since their decisions are made more or less by default, due to their perception of rules. Most people, however, operate between the extremes of rigid adherence to rules, on the one hand, and flagrant defiance, on the other. Rather than view the world in black-and-white terms, most of us see everyday situations in shades of gray. Because of this complexity, we are continually faced with decisions. If we're in a hurry, we might turn right on red even though there's a sign prohibiting it. When we refuse someone's invitation to a party, we might say that we have already made plans even though we haven't.

Many of our decisions tend to be influenced by the situation. Suppose, for example, that you've made your grocery list and vow to stick to it. Then at the store you notice a half-price sale on ice cream. "That's too good to pass up," you say to yourself, even though you're on a diet. "I'd better buy some. I need to be prepared in case company drops in." As another example, suppose you're driving to work and suddenly someone cuts in front of you. The right thing to do would be to give the other driver some extra room, but you also have the urge to display your annoyance. Which do you choose?

Your decision will be determined by the relative strength of the forces within you. One part of you is aware of the "right" thing to do, but another part of you experiences urges and feelings that demand to be satisfied. There is also a third force that tries to allow self-expression while convincing yourself that you're operating within the rules. Some people call this the voice of reason.

In this example of the driver cutting in front of you, you probably experience a number of things: anger at the other driver, annoyance at yourself for getting angry, and a voice of reason in the back of your mind trying to convince you to calm down. How you react will depend on which force is strongest at that moment. If your anger is strongest, you will honk your horn, tailgate, or make rude hand gestures. If your annoyance at yourself is strongest, you will meekly slow down but, perhaps, remain feeling unsettled. If your voice of reason wins out, you will probably slow down and turn your thoughts to something else, leaving the situation comfortably behind you.

In this example, you can probably recognize which force is most like the inner brat. It's the part of you that has the urge to make the other driver suffer for what he did to you. We all have such feelings, but we don't always act on them. That is because, as human beings, our brain has developed far beyond the point of reacting impulsively to anything and everything.

Modern research has contributed a great deal of knowledge about how the brain works, especially in relation to physical functioning. Certain areas of the brain have been identified as controlling specific parts of the body. For example, scientists have identified the parts of the brain that control speech, hearing, and vision. Many seizure disorders have been linked to particular areas of the brain. From studies of people with brain injuries, we know that certain lesions in the brain result in corresponding difficulties with movement, perception, or judgment. Recently there have been developments in identifying certain parts of the brain that are associated with conscience as well as with anger and other strong emotions.

But brain science is still in its infancy. Despite advances in techniques for viewing the brain and measuring its activity, there is still no definitive answer about how the *mind* works. The mind cannot be measured by x-rays, CAT scans, or MRIs.[6] Two people may have injuries in the same part of the brain, yet their reactions and behaviors will not be identical. No one has yet found a way to measure intelligence or personality directly. IQ tests and personality tests do not measure actual traits; they measure only responses that are assumed to be related to the traits in question. However, despite the fact that we still have much to learn about the mind, we have come a long way since philosophers began speculating about it centuries ago.

Historical Perspective on the Study of the Mind

The mind has been studied and speculated about at least as far back as ancient Greek and Roman written history. Until the last couple of centuries, most philosophers, theologians, and physicians attributed abnormal or undesirable behavior to external forces, such as demons or displeasure of the gods. One notable exception was Hippocrates, a Greek physician who lived around 400 B.C. He described four "humors," or bodily fluids: blood, black bile, yellow bile, and phlegm. According to Hippocrates, mental problems were presumed to result from an imbalance among these humors. Thus, melancholia (a chronic state of sadness) was assumed to stem from an excess of black bile. Changeable temperament was attributed to too much blood. Sluggishness supposedly originated from a preponderance of phlegm, and irritability and anxiety were said to come from too much yellow bile.

In the Middle Ages, witchcraft and demonology had a strong influence in society. People who committed crimes or acted in unusual ways were said to be possessed or cursed. It is from these times that we have the common excuse, "The devil made me do it."

It was not until the late nineteenth century that the workings of the mind were studied systematically. Sigmund Freud (1856–1939), a neurologist in Vienna, studied hypnosis, which was at the height of popularity at that time. In a trance state, people often performed acts or reported things that they claimed they did not voluntarily set out to do. (Some stage productions and films of so-called hypnotized subjects imply that the hypnotist has a magical control over the person in the trance. In actuality, no one can be forced to perform acts under hypnosis that they would not do when in a normal, waking state.) Freud noted that, even when people weren't hypnotized, they could not always explain why they did or felt certain things. In other words, their motives were outside their conscious awareness.

Freud devoted his life to developing his theory of psychoanalysis, which dominated Western European and American societies for the first half of the twentieth century. Since then, many experts have criticized his work, primarily because his theories have never been "proven." Nevertheless, he has left a legacy that has influenced not only psychotherapy and medicine but also cultural values. His major contribution was to introduce the idea that personality and behavior are determined by powerful inner forces. He inspired not only professionals but people in general to look beneath the obvious, to speculate on people's defense mechanisms and hidden agendas.

It is beyond the scope of this book to delve into psychoanalytic theory. For our purposes, it is relevant to address the mind's internal forces, because the inner brat has roots in such forces. I will briefly describe some aspects of psychological theories that emphasize the role of unconscious motives. Keep in mind that these are theories, not facts. They provide a framework for describing feelings and motivations that cannot be observed or measured directly. These theories are useful for understanding ourselves from various points of view, but by no means do they explain or predict *all* human feelings and actions.

Freud's theory of psychoanalysis is quite complex. As a basis for understanding the inner brat, we need only address his description of the major components of the mind. Freud stated that the mind consists of three major forces. Students of psychology will recognize the terms *id*, *ego*, and *superego*. These forces, which are said to be fueled by our mental, or *psychic*, energy, interact with one another. According to Freud, these forces work unconsciously, below our level of awareness.

A Simplified Illustration of Freud's View of the Mind

A convenient way of depicting Freud's theory of mental forces is via comparison with characters in the popular children's television program *Sesame Street*. I don't know whether the creators of this show were aware that certain characters reflected Freud's concepts, but they are remarkably representative. Let's examine them now.

Freud observed that, within us all, there is a basic, primitive drive to satisfy our urges, to maximize pleasure and minimize pain. He called this the id. The id is approximated in the character Cookie Monster of *Sesame Street*. Cookie Monster is pure impulse, with only one goal in mind—to get cookies. Being a children's program, *Sesame Street* keeps this creature quite gentle, but you can imagine what would happen if Cookie Monster got angry. He could be a real brat. Thus, our inner brat is somewhat like Cookie Monster, but it is more like a Cookie Monster with an attitude.

In opposition to our id is Freud's concept of the superego. The superego is embodied in the *Sesame Street* character Bert. Bert represents the stern father figure, for whom society's rules are very important. We all have a bit of Bert in us. It's called values, morals, or conscience. The superego is the part of our personality that keeps us ethical, the part of us that knows right from wrong and guides us in decisions. The superego is always trying to hold the impulses of the id in check.

Finally, there is the ego, which serves as mediator between the id and the superego. It tries to gratify the primitive urges of the id but in a manner that is acceptable to the limits imposed by the superego. The *Sesame Street* character that best defines the ego is Bert's sidekick, Ernie. Ernie is a playful character who tries to get what he wants, but not in an unbridled, impetuous way. To meet his desires, he uses compromise, so he stays within the spirit of the law as defined by Bert, even if he fudges on the letter of the law. An example of Ernie as ego occurred on a recent episode of *Sesame Street*. *Bert* is in a bad mood, but Ernie is in such a good mood he wants to sing. Bert turns to Ernie and says, "Do me a favor, Ernie. Don't sing." Then Ernie playfully responds, "What if I just hum a little?"

The action of the ego is also revealed in the old joke about the father who, upon catching his son playing with his genitals, warned him that this would make him blind. So the son retorted, "How about if I just do it till I need glasses?"

In summary, our inner brat has roots in a primitive force that demands immediate gratification without regard for the consequences. This is the force that often gets us into trouble with ourselves and other people. Conscience and morals serve to keep this brat in check, but as we know from experience, they are not always successful at doing so. In a mature person, the mediating influence of the ego can often find a way to express urges and impulses in a manner that is not destructive.

We all have these three forces within us. These forces are *dynamic*. That is, they are always in flux, vying for control. Whenever we respond to a situation, we consciously or unconsciously decide which force is going to win. Will it be our impulse? Will it be "the right thing to do"? Will it be something in between?

Let's consider an example. Suppose a co-worker at the office says something that makes you absolutely furious. You have several options. Your first impulse might be to punch that person in the face. That would be the preference of your id, or your inner brat. However, your superego, or your "Bert," would frown on such behavior, so you might therefore choose to say nothing. Alternatively, you might say to yourself, "That person really made me mad. I can't just sit here and do nothing." So you say something sarcastic, which conveys anger within a thin veil of civility. Thus, you've channeled that urge to strike into something more socially acceptable.

Although we all know right from wrong, it's not always easy to follow the rules to the letter. For example, we know we shouldn't lie. But what do you do if your hostess at a dinner party asks you, "How do you like my tofu-sardine soufflé?"—and you hate it? Somewhere in there we need to weigh what is right and wrong against what is desired. And in this case you would probably value interpersonal harmony over telling the truth. So while you wouldn't impulsively blurt out, "This is the most vile thing I've ever eaten," neither would you say, "It's absolutely delicious." Instead, you might hedge: "It's very interesting," or "You sure know how to come up with original dishes."

Other Theories of the Mind

Although Freud was the most familiar figure of early psychoanalysis, he was not the only one to propose unconscious forces of the mind. Carl Jung, a contemporary of Freud, also presented the idea of the unconscious. But Jung's view of the unconscious was different. From his studies of philosophy, religion, myths, and symbols, as well as from his observations of mental patients, he concluded that certain predispositions and tendencies are inherited from past generations and are present in all people. Jung referred to this as the "collective unconscious." The collective unconscious consists of units called *archetypes*, which are collections of tendencies to react to certain things and events in certain ways. For example, the "mother" archetype is the cumulative experience of our ancestors' responses to mothers, grandmothers, stepmothers, etc. When you think of the term *mother*, you have an immediate sense of what that means—good and bad. According to Jung, babies are born with an internalized archetype of the mother, such that they somehow intuitively know what a mother is and what to expect from her.

Jung described several archetypes, including the Mother, the Hero, the Child, the Trickster, and the Shadow. Of particular interest here is the Shadow, the archetype that typifies the animal instincts of human nature. It is the repository of unacceptable motives and tendencies, the side of ourselves that we prefer not to recognize. To some extent, the Shadow archetype resembles both Freud's concept of the id and our current notion of the inner brat.

In the 1950s, the psychiatrist Eric Berne developed the theory of Transactional Analysis. He also embraced the idea of unconscious forces and images in the mind, but he presented them in terms of how the individual interacts with other people. Berne proposed three major states of mind, called *ego states*, which are not identical to Freud's definition of the ego.

These ego states are sets of behavior patterns associated with corresponding feelings. Berne identified three main patterns: the Parent, the Adult, and the Child. Each ego state encompasses a cluster of thoughts and emotions, a vocabulary, a voice, a posture, and other behavioral characteristics. The Parent ego state comprises the rules and values of one's own parents and caretakers. The Adult ego state functions somewhat like an objective computer, logically appraising situations and predicting outcomes. The Child ego state represents archaic elements that are present from one's own childhood. Berne described two types of Child states: the *adapted child*, who behaves in accordance with the parents' wishes; and the *natural child*, who wants to be spontaneous and/or creative. We each carry all of these ego states within us, with one of them predominant at any given time.

To some extent, Berne's theory resembles that of Freud. His Child ego state resembles the id. His Adult ego state is similar to Freud's concept of the ego. His Parent ego state is reminiscent of Freud's superego. Also, like Freud, Berne presumed that the three ego states interact with one another and that emotional problems result when they are out of balance. For example, the Adult ego state is usually considered the most mature. However, a person who is always logical and objective—like Mr. Spock from *Star Trek*—lacks creativity and enjoyment in life. On the other hand, a person who demands freedom of expression and lives from moment to moment in the Child ego state is erratic, unstable, and lacks long-term satisfaction. When the moral, rule-bound Parent ego state predominates, a person can become quite rigid and intolerant.

While there are similarities in how Berne and Freud viewed the mind, Berne disagreed with Freud's assertion that the forces within the mind are unconscious. Berne maintained that we can be aware of which ego state we're in. Many of us know quite well when we're behaving in the spontaneous manner of our Child state, when we're being bossy or opinionated in our Parent state, and when we're using the logical thinking of our Adult state.

The inner brat is also a state of which we're usually aware. The inner brat is most similar to Berne's *spontaneous* Child ego state, but in this case, the spontaneity is expressed as impulsiveness. When we reflect on our own behavior, we can usually identify when we've been "bratty." Also, consistent with Berne's emphasis on interpersonal interaction, the inner brat often expresses itself most strongly in relation to other people. Recall the case of Emily, who had a problem with her temper and took out her anger on her family.

The theories presented above are different ways of understanding how the mind functions. Rather than attributing our thoughts and actions to external elements or demons, we can envision actual internal forces that interact with one another. It's convenient to have labels for these forces, but it's also important to remember that the labels are based on theories, not on specifically identifiable parts of the brain. The inner brat is also just a convenient label to encapsulate a set of thoughts, feelings, and behaviors. As we shall see later, there are some unconscious elements assumed in this label, but most of the time the inner brat is available to our conscious awareness.

Newer Approaches to the Mind and Its Workings

More and more, mental-health experts recognize that while our minds encompass memories and motivations that we're not aware of, we are not at the mercy of involuntary mental forces. Empirical research has demonstrated that we have plenty of conscious awareness and capacity for self-direction. Now, not only can we understand ourselves better, but we can also do something to change disturbing thoughts, habits, and emotions.

One of the most successful techniques for helping people gain self-insight and learn better coping strategies is the *cognitive* approach. The basic premise of this approach is that it is not people or situations that make us upset, but, rather, it is the assumptions we make and what we say to ourselves about those situations.

For example, let's say you had agreed to meet someone for lunch, but she didn't show up. Your first inclination might be to feel angry after waiting more than half an hour, and you might stay angry for the rest of the day. Suppose, however, that your friend called you later that afternoon to apologize for standing you up, explaining that she was in a car accident and was taken by ambulance to the hospital. Would you still be angry then? Of course not. In the first scenario, the reason you were angry was because of *assumptions* you made about why she was late—assumptions that probably included words such as "inconsiderate," "rude," or other derogatory terms. Throw in a couple of phrases like "I refuse to be treated this way," and you set yourself up for resentment. However, in the second scenario, your assumptions changed. When you knew a different set of facts, you no longer attributed negative characteristics to your friend. Accordingly, you were no longer angry.

The cognitive approach to human problems has been proven effective in psychotherapy. In fact, in some studies it has been shown to be superior to antidepressant and antianxiety medication! It is a common-sense approach that puts you, not a therapist, in charge of your own self-improvement. One does not even have to be in therapy to learn and apply cognitive strategies. The majority of self-help books on the market today address problems from a cognitive point of view.

Cognitive techniques are not limited to the mental-health profession. Over three hundred years ago, Shakespeare's Hamlet uttered, "There is nothing either good or bad, but thinking makes it so."[7] Many philosophies and religions take the view that we make our own pleasure and suffering. One of the four "truths" of Buddhism, for example, is that our dissatisfactions arise within ourselves, out of ignorance, out of blindness to objective reality, or out of simple wanting. In modern life we are familiar with the expression, "It all depends upon your point of view."

Some people use cognitive mental strategies intuitively on a daily basis. They don't get upset easily; they roll with the punches and don't hold grudges. Do these people have fewer problems than the rest of us? Not likely. What they do have is a view of life that is realistic. They don't insist that everything must be perfect or that everyone must like them. They exemplify the expression, "When life gives you lemons, make lemonade." At the same time, they do not necessarily pretend that everything is wonderful. For these people, cognitive techniques come naturally. While we can't all be so intuitively adaptable, the good news is that it's not hard to learn.

One of the most prominent experts in the field of cognitively based techniques is Albert Ellis, Ph.D., founder of the school of Rational Emotive Behavioral Therapy (REBT). His techniques have been adopted by mental-health professionals all over the world. Dr. Ellis acknowledges that we are shaped by our past, but in order to put an end to emotional pain we must focus on the present. He concedes that many of our assumptions are not entirely within our awareness, but upon closer self-examination we can uncover them, dispute them, and replace dysfunctional beliefs and assumptions with more rational, realistic, and productive ones.

Ellis has outlined several "irrational beliefs" that distort people's perceptions. Some examples of irrational beliefs include the following:

- I need love and approval from those significant to me, and I must avoid disapproval from any source.

- My unhappiness is caused by things that are outside my control, so there is little I can do to feel any better.

- Things must be the way I want them to be; otherwise life will be intolerable.

- I shouldn't have to feel discomfort and pain. I can't stand them and must avoid them at all costs.

- Every problem should have an ideal solution, and it's intolerable when one can't be found.

Ellis also points out that, in addition to distorting our perceptions with irrational beliefs, we engage in certain thought processes that exaggerate annoyances into catastrophes. For example, when we label something as *awful* or *terrible*, of course it feels overwhelming. When we tell ourselves, "I can't stand it," or say, "He shouldn't be that way," we intensify our frustration.

It's not hard to recognize the inner brat in the preceding irrational beliefs and statements. Your inner brat is the part of you that makes demands; it wants what it wants, when it wants it, and doesn't care who or what is destroyed in the process. When you find yourself saying such negative things at the back of your mind, you can attribute this to the entity that I call the inner brat.

A slightly different twist on the cognitive approach is the Addictive Voice Recognition Technique introduced by Jack Trimpey, a former alcoholic.[8] Unlike many addicts who choose to believe they have an incurable disease over which they are powerless, Trimpey proposes that the mind can overcome even the worst of urges. Like Freud, he states that appetite and desire are very strong, primitive forces. In fact, he names these forces "The Beast." Trimpey points out that by discovering the Beast's mind tricks, one can overcome the forces and control one's own behavior.

The Beast, according to Trimpey, represents the primitive part of the brain, similar to the brain of lower animals. Its main concern is with physical survival through the pursuit of pleasure. When it finds pleasure in alcohol, tobacco, or tasty food, it demands more and more of the same. Among people who are addicted to a given substance, it is the Beast brain that is responsible. Trimpey notes that we also have a more advanced part of the brain—the cortex—which separates us from more primitive animals and can voluntarily override demands made by the Beast.

Trimpey shows readers how to recognize when the Beast is trying to take over. He describes the tricks that the Beast uses, such as pretending to be your friend, convincing you why you need a drink or a cigarette. It does not have your best welfare in mind, even though it pretends to do so. The Beast's messages are what Trimpey calls the "Addictive voice." The Beast is a sinister, dangerous part of your psyche that must be destroyed.

Like Trimpey's notion of the Beast, the inner brat also "talks" to you. But the inner brat is not necessarily evil or sinister, nor does it set out to harm you. The inner brat talks to you through irrational assumptions and beliefs. It certainly wants to maximize pleasure and avoid pain, and it will pester you as long as possible. Nevertheless, now that you have a better idea of how your brat operates, you are on your way to getting it under control.

This chapter summarizes some historical developments in how we view the mind. It is only in the last century that the mind has been studied systematically. The current popular view combines physiological and mental factors, both conscious and unconscious. The inner brat is a concept that derives from these established theories and methods.

5

When the Forces Are out of Balance: Impulsiveness

In the previous chapter, I described the mind as a mix of conscious and unconscious forces. These forces all work together to try to maintain a sense of balance or harmony. Without this balance, the inner brat is apt to emerge. Our impulses supersede our logic, and we end up doing and saying things that we later regret.

To illustrate this, I will first describe a bit of theoretical background and then show you how this fits with the inner-brat concept. Certain problems with impulse control are understandable in terms of both psychological and cultural factors.

Theoretical Considerations

Consider Freud's concepts of the id, superego, and ego. These represent our primitive appetites, our internalized knowledge of right and wrong, and our reasoning capabilities, respectively. We need all of these to function in the world. Similarly, Berne's ego states of Child, Parent, and Adult reflect the complexity of the human personality and its tendency to approach different types of situations in different ways. Jung, a contemporary of Freud, proposed the collective unconscious, in which are deposited our ancestors' proclivities to perceive and react in specific ways.

What all these theories have in common is the presumption that the underlying entities of our personalities are not inert and stationary but, rather, always in flux, competing with one another. For example, let's apply Berne's concepts to a situation where you are attending a play. Your Child ego state may react with wonder as the actors appear in their costumes. As you are drawn into the story portrayed on stage, the Child in you may gasp in suspense. At intermission, the Child might fade into the background, supplanted by the Parent or the Adult. Suppose you observe a group of people in the corner of the lobby, laughing raucously and jostling each other. If you regard them as behaving immaturely and observe them with disdain, it is your Parent ego state that perceives this. If you watch them with a detached attitude, wondering what the joke is, then it is your logical Adult ego state that is predominant at the time.

In a similar way, Freud described the human mind as a hydraulic system, with pressures of the id, superego, and ego shifting back and forth with one another for expression. Jung's archetypes (inherited emotional predispositions) are described in terms of opposites. For example, the Hero archetype is the opposite of the Demon. The Animus, or masculine archetype, is counterbalanced by the feminine Anima. Within the Mother archetype are both the kind, generous mother and the evil, witchlike mother. All of these archetypes find expression at various times in our lives and may even be in conflict with one another.

The experts all point out that there are many facets to our personalities, some of which we are aware, and others of which we are not aware. These facets fluctuate in their strength and in their subsequent expression in our thoughts, feelings, and behaviors. When one component predominates, the others stay in the background. When one of the background elements of the personality is triggered, it then takes over predominance. It is like a perpetual balancing act.

People's personalities differ from one another, partly because of how the various facets interact. Some people thrive on excitement and crisis, while others panic when faced with the unexpected. Some people are loud and boisterous, while others project a calm demeanor. Some people are more deliberate in their thinking, while others make snap decisions. Even though people have certain patterns and predilections, no one is virtually the same all the time. Even loud people are quiet some of the time. Even reticent people can sometimes rise to the occasion without flinching.

Although it's possible for us to behave in ways we're not used to, we don't feel comfortable doing so for very long. For example, consider the case of Trudy, who would describe herself as basically shy. She goes to a party and chats with other people. She puts on such a good performance that no one would guess that she's bashful. But at the end of the evening, Trudy is exhausted. It may take a couple of days before she feels up to socializing again.

On the other hand, Craig lives for social contact. He hates being alone, but a recent snowstorm and power outage keeps him isolated for two days with no phone, no e-mail, no contact. He tries to make the best of it, saying to himself, "This is a good time to catch up on my reading," but after an hour or so, he starts to get restless. He picks up the phone. Still dead. He looks out the window. Still snowing and blowing out there. No one is outside. By the time the storm lifts, Craig is the first one out the door in search of human interaction. Had Trudy been stuck in this situation, she would not have experienced nearly the same discomfort of being alone.

Although we *can* behave in ways that are not typical for us, it takes more effort. Therefore, we usually try to minimize how often and how long we do so. In general, we operate within a limited range of thoughts and behaviors that is comfortable for us. Depending on which central facet of the personality predominates, we see three basic approaches to dealing with the world

Some people focus on work and productivity most of the time. These are the people that Eric Berne would define as being predominantly in the Parent ego state. Freud might say they are controlled by their superego. In *Sesame Street* terms, these are the "Berts" of the world. Keep in mind that they are not always serious. They do have fun, but they gravitate back to seriousness as their default mode. In the extreme, some such individuals have difficulty relaxing and kicking back.

Other types enjoy a more relaxed approach to life. They're not as concerned about keeping to a strict schedule or making sure that rules are followed to the letter. Yet they can be rational and productive. When deadlines approach or when legal consequences loom, these people can buckle down and adhere to rigid standards, but as soon as the pressure is off, they resume their preferred mode of living. Such individuals are predominantly in the Adult ego state, as defined by Eric Berne.

A third mode of operating within the world is by responding to impulse. This mode is what Freud might describe as an id-dominated personality. As I mentioned in the last chapter, it is akin to *Sesame Street*'s Cookie Monster. Impulsive people don't think before they act or speak. They get themselves into hot water in relationships. They make commitments to themselves and others but don't keep them. They're not necessarily irresponsible or unkind—or at least they don't like to think of themselves as such. But because the balance of their mental forces is tipped toward spontaneity and because, like most people, these individuals always gravitate toward what feels like a normal balance for them, they will continue to repeat the same mistakes over and over. These are the people who are ruled by their inner brat.

Is It Hopeless?

I have just illustrated how we each operate within a limited range of thoughts, feelings, and behaviors that form the basis of a comfort level, or what I call our "cruising speed." We always tend to revert to this cruising speed. Does this mean that we're doomed to continue counterproductive habits?

The answer is both yes and no. I'd love to tell you that it's easy to change your personality, that you just need to follow three or seven or ten simple steps. I would love to tell you this, but I can't, because there is no such formula. And most people's personalities are pretty much set by the time they reach adolescence.

Nevertheless, it is possible to change certain thoughts and behaviors. It is also possible to make slight modifications so that what was once counterproductive now becomes useful. But it takes work.

Consider the case of Norman, an energetic young man, twenty-seven years old. As a child, Norman could never sit still in school. He would talk out in class. His hands were always busy fiddling with pens, papers, or rubber bands. Fortunately, he was a bright youngster and managed to graduate from high school with honors, despite the fact that he rarely completed his homework assignments on time. Norman went to college, but because he had never mastered good study skills, he flunked out in the first semester. Not surprised by this failure, he was nevertheless dejected, especially because he felt that he had disappointed his parents.

By the time Norman came to see me, he had been fired from several jobs, for various reasons, including chronic lateness, failure to turn in paperwork, and lack of attention to details. He had recently moved back home because he could not afford his own apartment. He complained that his parents were always asking him what he was going to do with his life and when was he going to finally grow up. Norman was angry with them but also angry with himself. He felt like a failure.

As Norman and I talked, I gradually learned more about him. Although he wasn't much of a reader, he did seem quite knowledgeable about current events. (He explained that he listened to news radio for several hours per day.) He had loads of friends, for whom he would drop everything if they needed help. He had lofty ideas for an international business but had not done anything to get started on it. We eventually got around to talking about what stood in the way of his success. Norman had

Stefan

a lot of excuses: he had no capital to start a business; no one wanted to give him a chance; he couldn't get past receptionists to talk to people who would be in a position to help him. All of these were external reasons. Norman blamed situations and other people for his lack of success.

Finally, I suggested that perhaps he himself might have something to do with it. He did acknowledge that he lacked discipline but expressed this almost with pride: "I'm not a nine-to-five person," he said indignantly. "I never have been and never will be." His attitude seemed to be "I'm not going to change, so the world must accommodate me." It was apparent that Norman had a strong inner brat that didn't like to be accountable to any-one. It just wanted to do what it wanted to do, when it wanted to do it. His inner brat was not malicious; it was merely undisciplined.

Over the next few weeks, Norman worked to tame his inner brat. He changed certain thoughts and behaviors, and he set up his work environment so that it would be conducive to a more disciplined approach to life while still allowing plenty of freedom to be spontaneous. It wasn't easy. In fact, for the first few weeks, Norman complained that he felt "artificial." But as he saw positive results toward getting his business off the ground, he found it easier to stay on course.

Norman hadn't transformed his personality. He was still the same fun-loving, helpful guy that everyone liked, but now he was not so ready to dismiss certain traits as unchangeable. Furthermore, he assumed more responsibility for his actions and enjoyed the benefits of achieving one small goal after another. Norman was still himself, but he was a more grown-up version of himself. He had been dominated by his inner brat, but he eventually learned to take charge. The inner brat didn't disappear.

On a daily basis, Norman still had to be aware of how it influenced his decisions and behavior. At first, he felt exhausted from his efforts to exert control. But within a short time, his inner brat settled down.

Every so often Norman lapses into old impulsive habits, especially when he is overly stressed or when he is tempted by what seems to be an irresistible distraction. However, now that he knows that his impulsiveness is just the product of the little brat inside him, it's a lot easier for him to get back on track.

Some experts might label Norman as having attention deficit disorder. Indeed, he does meet many of the criteria, including excessive distractibility, inattention, and general restlessness. Some mental-health practitioners, upon noticing such symptoms, would have immediately suggested medication to help Norman "calm down." I did not rule out referring him to a physician for medication evaluation, but I first wanted to see how well he could learn to impose self-control. Norman was motivated to do so, and he needed to acquire a few skills, but once he started practicing, he no longer exhibited the typical behavior pattern of attention deficit disorder.

Attention Deficit Disorder

Attention deficit disorder, which is also known as attention deficit hyperactivity disorder, or ADHD, is a common diagnosis for people who have a great deal of trouble focusing attention and sustaining effort. Many of them also are excessively fidgety and restless and have been since early childhood. ADHD is more than just normal childhood distractibility. It is commonly believed that there is an underlying physical cause, and although brain activity among some ADHD children is different from that of normal children, evidence is still inconclusive about the specific physical cause.

The current *Diagnostic and Statistical Manual* of the American Psychiatric Association (DSM IV) estimates that 3 percent to 5 percent of school-age children have ADHD, but many more than that are given the ADHD diagnosis. In some schools in the United States, as many as 20 percent of students have been so diagnosed.

According to Dr. Lawrence Diller, author of *Running on Ritalin*, stimulant medication (the most common of which is methylphenidate, marketed as Ritalin) for ADHD is given ten times more often to American children than to those of Europe and industrialized Asia. Since 1990 there has been a 700 percent increase in the number of Ritalin prescriptions written in the United States. Eighty-five percent of the world's stimulants are sold in the United States.[9]

Why the sudden surge in stimulant use? Because it works. Just about anyone who takes Ritalin or other stimulants will experience improved attention. You don't have to have ADHD to get this benefit. The downside is that there are many possible side effects, some of them serious. Nervousness and difficulty sleeping are the most common, but a person may also have skin rashes, stomach problems, headaches, unwanted weight loss, heart palpitations, and irregular heartbeats. Children who use stimulants sometimes have delayed growth. Furthermore, with long-term use you may need to keep increasing the dosage to get the therapeutic effect.

Before you call your doctor to get a pill to combat your impulsive behavior or your disorganized life, first see what you can do on your own by taming your inner brat. It worked for Norman. And it may be all that you need.

Diagnosing ADHD

No one knows for sure why so many kids are labeled as hyperactive, but a major reason is that diagnostic criteria are not precise. There is no definitive test for ADHD. Diagnosis is a process of carefully reviewing a child's history and family environment as well as ruling out other possible reasons for hyperactivity or distractibility, such as medical problems or anxiety. Parents and teachers may be asked to complete behavioral questionnaires, and the child may be given some intellectual and/or personality tests to help rule out learning disabilities or underlying emotional issues. All of these approaches considered together will help determine whether a child has ADHD, but the evaluation is still somewhat subjective and depends a great deal on the clinician's biases and experiences.

Thus, two professionals might examine the same child but arrive at different conclusions. One might determine that the child does have ,ADHD, while the other might view the symptoms as similar to ADHD but not extreme enough to justify the diagnosis. After all, what child isn't restless, distractible, and impulsive? Some are more so than others. Those in the extreme we call ADHD, but there is no professional agreement about what constitutes the cutoff point.

In addition to imprecise diagnostic criteria, contemporary treatment philosophies seek medical explanations for all problems, including emotional and behavioral problems. However, in looking for the biological marker, researchers often disregard important environmental and social conditions that promote distractibility and poor attention span. These will be discussed later in this chapter.

Impulse-Control Problems and Self-Esteem

ADHD is one of many disorders that result from poor impulse control. There is some research evidence that extreme impulsiveness is caused by chemical reactions in the brain. So far, however, no single chemical that explains the range of impulse-control problems has been isolated. Besides, just about everything we do, think, and feel is either the result or cause of some chemical reaction in our body.

The inner brat is at the heart of many problems that mental-health professionals call impulse-control disorders or problems with self-regulation. People who have such problems typically don't anticipate the consequences of their actions, or if they do anticipate the consequences, they don't give them much weight. They have trouble with self-discipline. Like Norman, they may have plans but don't follow through with them. The sad part is that they end up depriving themselves of opportunities to feel competent and successful.

When you feel incompetent and unsuccessful day after day, your self-esteem suffers. Low self-esteem reduces your tolerance for frustration, which, in turn, lowers your motivation to persist when things get tough.

Consider the case of Steve, father of two children, ages seven and four. Recently Steve and his family spent the day at a nearby amusement park. The day started off fine. But at lunchtime Steve lost his temper. The incident seemed to be a minor one, but it was not the first time that Steve had reacted angrily to something trivial.

Here's what had happened. While he stayed with the kids at a picnic table, his wife went to the snack bar to buy lunch for everyone. Steve had asked her to bring him a hot dog. When his wife returned with four corn dogs, he was livid. "I told you I wanted a hot dog!" he shouted. "I'm sorry," answered his wife. "I thought you said 'corn dog.' But why don't you eat it anyway? We hardly ever have these things, so we might as well enjoy them." But Steve was relentless. He ate the corn dog but complained the whole time. Although his wife offered to get him a hot dog in addition, he just growled that the food at this park was already overpriced and that he wasn't going to throw any more money away because of her stupidity. Steve could not shake his anger all afternoon, barking at the children when they asked for a drink or said they needed to use the restroom. The family ended up leaving early and driving home in silence.

Steve's inner brat was triggered by his frustration: he expected one thing for lunch and ended up with something else. This frustration led to his impulsive aggression toward his family, which ruined the afternoon for everyone. We all get irritated at times and overreact to situations. For Steve, however, this irritation is almost a weekly occurrence. Afterwards he apologizes and promises himself and his wife that he won't do this again. But the next time he is frustrated, Steve seems to forget to control his quicksilver temper.

Steve's temper was not caused by the corn dog. It goes much deeper than that. The corn-dog incident was just the trigger. Although no one knows it, Steve is disappointed with himself. He had pictured fatherhood as a "buddy trip" with his children. Now they are afraid of him. He doesn't feel at all successful as a father. Thus, when it's time to act like one and be part of the family, he makes very little effort. To cope, he has begun spending more and more time at work, and so his outbursts are less frequent, but he's no closer to being the father he wants to be.

Like Steve, we all have our outbursts at times. But when overreaction gets to be a habit, we have let our inner brat control us more than is good for us.

Not all impulsiveness is bad. Sometimes it's useful not to have to stop and think about things. For example, if you have to protect yourself from an assailant running toward you, you don't have much time to plan a strategy. Or if you get excited when your team scores a goal, you will lose your spontaneous enthusiasm if you think too long about what to yell.

The reason you can act so quickly in such situations is that your behavior is not inhibited or suppressed by counteracting tendencies. When being chased by an assailant, the first and foremost thing on your mind is to get away. Even if you have a pain in your leg or you're short of breath, these discomforts will not slow you down much when your life is in danger. On the other hand, if you're just out for your morning jog and pain strikes, you will notice it more and perhaps even slow down because of it. The pain inhibits your running. It all depends on what's more important at the time.

We all have impulses, both positive and negative. The negative impulses include destructive behaviors, such as eating, drinking, or smoking too much, spending money carelessly, and losing one's temper. People who have such problems have not mastered inhibition or regulation of their impulses. Freud might say that they have an inadequate superego. Berne would describe them as having a Child-dominated personality. I view this problem with inhibition as emanating from the inner brat.

Regardless of theoretical definitions, the hallmark of impulsive behavior is that certain inhibitions are lacking. Usually, when we're about to say or do something inappropriate, we stop ourselves. A man may look at an attractive woman and think, "Boy would I like to get ahold of her," but he doesn't usually say it out loud, nor does he act on it, because other parts of his mind act as a censor to inhibit the words and actions. Similarly, someone who is determined to quit smoking may think, "I would really like a cigarette," but will not reach for one, despite the cravings.

Acting on impulse means acting without anticipating the consequences of one's actions. People whose lives are ruled by impulse fail to pay attention to certain subtleties and cues in their environment, such that they repeatedly make illogical decisions. Not only do they have problems with continuing bad habits, but they often have difficulties in close relationships. They may even get into trouble with the law.

Much research demonstrates that people who are able to resist impulse are generally happier and more successful in life. In his book *Emotional Intelligence*, psychologist Daniel Goleman describes a simple experiment conducted on four-year-olds by Walter Mischel and his colleagues. These children were left alone in a room with a marshmallow. They were told that either they could eat the marshmallow right away, or if they waited until the adult returned, they could have two marshmallows. Experimenters watched through a one-way mirror and recorded the children's actions. Years later, not only did those children who waited for the second marshmallow get into fewer fights at school and reach their goals more often, but their SATs (college-entrance exams) averaged 210 points higher (of a possible 1600) than those children who ate their marshmallow immediately.[10]

The ability to inhibit impulses is part of what Goleman calls emotional intelligence. People with a high emotional-intelligence quotient (EQ) are more aware of their feelings and impulses and are better able to regulate them. These people certainly experience frustration, but they are not overwhelmed by it. They set goals and work toward them, even in the face of obstacles. People with a high EQ are in control of their inner brats.

Cultural Factors That Contribute to Impulsiveness

Earlier, in the section on ADHD, I speculated that the rise in frequency of this diagnosis is due partly to the imprecision of the diagnosis as well as to a predilection for medical explanations of abnormal behavior. However, cultural factors are equally, if not more, important in accounting for the fact that people seem to have shorter attention spans, less patience, more frustration, and shorter fuses. The media that infiltrates our lives encourages certain expectations and experiences. We have become a culture of short attention span and immediate gratification.

The Short-Attention-Span Culture

Turn on any television program for children or teens, and the pace can make you dizzy. Scenes and images change rapidly, some flashing on the screen for only a second or two at a time. The entertainment industry presents this rapid pace on purpose. Research has shown that people pay attention to change. They are more alert in a changing environment and are more apt to pay attention to commercial advertising when it is intense with color, sound, and movement. The younger generation has come to expect rapid change and constant stimulation. Perhaps these expectations explain why ADHD diagnoses have been on the rise in recent years. People don't have a long attention span because they've been fed a diet of sound bites and image clips, T-shirt slogans, and one-liner jokes.

The Culture of Instant Gratification

Back in the days of the Pony Express, it took several weeks for a letter to travel from New York to San Francisco. Today, with e-mail and fax machines, it's there in a matter of seconds. Not too many years ago, when you ordered something through the mail, you were prepared to wait a month to have it delivered. Today you can have it within hours. For instance, at some merchant Web sites on the Internet, if you place your order before midnight, you'll get it the next morning. Eating out used to mean spending an hour and a half in a restaurant. You expected to wait at least twenty minutes for your meal. Nowadays, fast food has changed all that. You can get lunch within a minute or two, and you don't even have to leave your car.

We have come to expect instant service as the norm. Waiting ten minutes for food at McDonald's seems like an eternity. If someone doesn't instantly respond to an e-mail, we become impatient. And while we might be willing to wait up to a week for that CD we ordered online, we're not happy about it.

Although it's convenient to have information and consumer goods within easy reach, we begin to expect instant satisfaction and resolution within all areas of our life. Speed is the standard by which we measure progress. Recently, while listening to the radio, I heard a commercial for a revolutionary garage-door opener, which opens so fast that it saves you *up* to six seconds of time! If six seconds makes that much difference in getting your garage door open, then either you need to make more room in your schedule or you have problems way beyond the scope of this book.

Quick and Easy Is Best

Not only do we expect immediate satisfaction, we also expect ourselves and others to react quickly. People with quick reflexes are revered and rewarded. Sports heroes, game-show contestants, and pizza-delivery services all receive recognition for their speedy reactions.

We also expect to acquire knowledge and expertise with minimal effort. A cursory search on Amazon.com for book titles with words such as "instant," "minute," and "quick and easy" yielded thousands of such titles in print. Some current ones include *Instant Emotional Healing; The One-Minute Manager; One-Minute Wisdom; The Instant Millionaire; Marriage Made Simple; The Instant Juggling Book; The Five-Day Miracle Diet; Gotta Minute? The Ultimate Guide of One-Minute Workouts for Anyone, Anywhere, Anytime!; Ten Days to Self-Esteem;* and *Toilet Training in Less Than a Day.* These books imply that not only *can* we become experts, but we *should* be able to do so in a very short time. I imagine that there are countless disappointed and frustrated readers who did not achieve the desired results in the time promised. Also, note the popularity of what I call "Cliff Notes of Life." These are the collections of pithy sayings and little stories that teach a lesson or make a point. Titles such as *Don't Sweat the Small Stuff* and *Chicken Soup for the Soul* meet the demands of people who want to find the meaning of life but would rather absorb it in digest form than discover it for themselves.

Quick-and-easy books are also marketed to professionals. Frankly, it is not exactly reassuring to think that the guy who's remodeling my kitchen needs to consult *Quick and Basic Electricity*, or that my doctor may rely on books such as *The Five-Minute Pediatric Consult* or *The Five-Minute Emergency Medicine Consult*. I just hope they don't come up with titles like *Surgery for Dummies*.

What does all this emphasis on speed and high expectations have on our psyches? We are more stressed, more prone not only to frustration but to error. Try this simple experiment: copy any two consecutive sentences from this book. Just write with a pen as you normally do. Then call someone into the room to watch you write the same two sentences. The second time, write as quickly as you can. Instruct the other person to carefully scrutinize your facial expression, the way you hold the pen, and the degree of pressure you apply when writing. After you've completed this exercise, compare your two writing samples. If you're like most people, the second sample, which was produced under mild stress (i.e., being watched, hurrying) will look sloppier and less fluid.

When people are stressed, they are more likely to express frustration when making errors. If you've ever played sports, you can probably relate to this tendency. Imagine the tennis player who keeps missing one ball after another. The first miss may not bother her, but after three or four, she starts to stomp around the court more. Such stomping borders on bratty behavior.

Psychologists define frustration as what happens when an expected outcome fails to occur. It's bad enough to be frustrated, but research has shown that, in addition, the more frustrated we get, the more angry or aggressive we become.

With our current culture emphasizing speed, high expectations, and immediate gratification, people get more frustrated, more often. And because frustration usually generates aggression, we see more and more people angry at themselves and at others. Such conditions are bound to contribute to a major brat epidemic.

We have come to assume and take for granted that we should be entertained and stimulated, that we should never have to wait, and that skills should come easily. Furthermore, if life isn't easy, we're entitled to complain or even to have a tantrum. Unless we recognize the impulsive side of our inner brat, we will continue to feel dissatisfied and frustrated.

You, the reader, are by now familiar with your inner brat, but it's not enough just to recognize it. You must work to tame it. Unlike the book titles I mentioned, the problem with your inner brat will not be solved in one minute, or ten days, or six easy steps. Such thinking is the product of the culture in which we live. No, it will take time. But don't despair. The process is gradual but definitely cumulative. That is, each step you take adds up, and soon you'll be able to look back and see how far you've come.

Controlling your impulses is an important step toward taming your inner brat, but that's not enough. You must also learn to recognize a part of yourself that you may not like. In the next chapter, you will encounter the underlying source of your inner brat: narcissism.

6

Narcissism: The Basis of Brat Dominance

The word *brat* conjures up the image of a self-centered child whose sole purpose is to satisfy every whim and to grab attention at every opportunity. Brats are overly focused on themselves and, by definition, inconsiderate of others. They also have an exaggerated sense of entitlement. They believe that they are special and that they deserve to have whatever they want, whenever they want it. At the same time, they feel no particular obligation to consider other people's needs.

While being self-centered is quite common for a very young child, it is not acceptable for an adult. When an adult continually demands special treatment and is insensitive to the needs of others, mental-health experts describe such a person as *narcissistic*. The terms *narcissism* and *narcissistic* originate from Greek mythology. According to this story, Narcissus, a handsome young man, was obsessed with his own beauty. After he rejected the love of a nymph named Echo—who was so hurt that she faded away, except for her voice—the gods punished Narcissus by making him fall in love with his own reflection in a pool of water. Narcissus was so taken by this reflection that he drowned in pursuit of his own image in the water.

Today, narcissism refers to excessive self-concern and a sense of specialness, uniqueness, and entitlement. While narcissistic people seem to project an air of superiority and arrogance, they are not necessarily as confident as they appear. Some psychological experts propose that underneath the overconfident exterior lies much insecurity. Narcissists cannot tolerate even mild criticism because it threatens their fundamentally fragile self-esteem. When criticized, they are deeply hurt, and they overreact, sometimes with rage. Thus, narcissistic individuals may seem like a paradox: self-assured and demanding at one moment, and wounded victims the next. This paradoxical behavior stems from their excessive preoccupation with their own desires and feelings.

Jake

After being caught embezzling from his boss, Jake was referred to me by his attorney. He didn't think he needed a "shrink," but his lawyer suggested that since it was Jake's first offense, the judge might give him a lighter sentence if he voluntarily entered psychotherapy. His "assignment" was to explore the psychological reasons why he would steal from his employer of five years.

When Jake walked into my office, you'd never guess that he didn't want to be there. A handsome, well-dressed man, wearing just a touch of expensive cologne, he made a good first impression. He was friendly and soft-spoken, and he made good eye contact. As he sat down, he commented on how pleasant my office was and asked a few questions about some pictures on the wall. He then asked me how long I had been in practice and where I had gone to school. Just as he started inquiring about my family, I stopped him. "Thank you for your interest," I fired back as diplomatically as I could, "but this isn't a social visit. We're here to discuss you." As soon as I changed the discussion to the reason why he was there, it became apparent that Jake preferred to be the one asking the questions.

He did admit "transferring money" out of the business, using some elaborate scheme, but he insisted that he had intended to pay it back. Never once did he use the terms "embezzlement" or "stealing" or even "borrowing." Whenever he referred to his legal case, he used terms like "the situation" and "when all this happened to me." Jake couldn't understand why his boss was so angry with him. After all, he had apologized over and over. What more did the guy want? "Of course the money will be paid back," he added. (Note that he didn't say, "I will pay back the money.") *passive voice*

I saw Jake two more times before his sentencing. At these sessions, he spoke dramatically about his impoverished childhood and his abusive father and about how he managed to rise above it, to become student-body president of his high school and quarterback of the football team. He never had problems getting dates. In fact, girls used to throw themselves at him, and still did. Jake stated that he didn't go to college because he didn't need to. Making money was never a problem, and he couldn't see the point of "wasting four years reading dead people's books." Since the age of nineteen, he had worn designer clothes, driven fast cars, and eaten at expensive restaurants.

"I never had these things when I was growing up," he said softly. "I worked hard for them and I deserve them." He continued, "When business started slowing down, I still had my car payments and my credit cards. I certainly couldn't afford to ruin my credit rating. So there was no other choice but to work out a way to transfer funds out of the company just until business picked up again. If the economy hadn't slowed down all of a sudden, none of this would have happened to me."

Jake wasn't really interested in learning more about his mind and its workings. He never allowed me to probe beyond what he was prepared to tell me. I suspected that he was also using drugs, but he dismissed my questioning as preposterous. It was clear that the only reason Jake was seeing me was because of his attorney's suggestion that it might help for his sentencing. At his last visit, a few days before the sentencing hearing, he asked me to write a letter to the judge. "This is what I want you to say," he commanded. "Tell him that what happened to me was just a slipup. It won't happen again, because I've learned my lesson. Oh—and add something about my poor childhood, to get the judge's sympathy." I replied firmly that I couldn't write such a letter, since he didn't really seem committed to changing himself but just wanted to minimize the consequences of his previous actions.

Suddenly, Jake's charming manner evaporated. "I thought you were supposed to help me," he sneered. "These sessions were a total waste, then. I can't believe you would do such a thing to me! Here I am, trying to cooperate, answering your stupid questions, and you won't write one ******* letter! You know I'm not the 'jail' type!" Jake was enraged. He stormed out of the office—without paying his bill, I might add—and I never saw him again.

A few weeks later I learned that he had been sentenced to fifteen months in prison. I wouldn't be surprised if he got all his fellow prisoners to believe that he was there because of some terrible miscarriage of justice.

By this point Jake's inner brat should be obvious to you. He was extremely narcissistic, justifying his immoral behavior and expressing surprise when I didn't go along with it. According to him, it was necessary to steal from his employer because he needed to preserve his own expensive lifestyle, which he had "worked so hard" to attain. Jake's early show of interest and concern was simply manipulation to try to win me over. As soon as he realized that it wasn't getting the results he wanted, he saw no reason to be civil.

The Origins of Narcissism

Jake's case of narcissism is extreme. It is not typical. But we all have narcissistic tendencies to some extent. As infants, each one of us was self-absorbed. Our main concerns were whether we were hungry, wet, cold, or alone. Since we had no means of taking care of these needs ourselves, we were dependent on a parent or other caregiver to provide for us. Furthermore, since we had not developed language at that stage in our lives, the only way to communicate that we needed something was to cry or fuss. This behavior usually got someone's attention fairly soon.

As we grew older, we had to learn to wait for attention and satisfaction of physical needs. It was not always possible for our parents to take care of us immediately. For example, if we were out in public and decided we were hungry, it would take some time for our parent to bring us to a place where we could be fed. If we woke up from a nap, our wails weren't always heard right away. Thus, most of us learned to wait, trusting that help would be coming eventually.

Nevertheless, some remnants of that desperate need for immediate gratification remain in the recesses of our minds. When we are frustrated or stressed, this need tends to reemerge. Think of the times you have thought to yourself, "I can't stand this!" or "Make it stop!" At such times you feel essentially the same way you did as an infant when your diaper was wet and uncomfortable.

You probably don't remember how important and critical it seemed when your diaper was wet, but if you've observed babies in a similar situation, you can get a general idea. When an infant is uncomfortable, it becomes overwhelmed by frustration. That's all the infant can think about. If you try to distract the baby, it may stop fussing, but only momentarily. Not until the baby is rid of that uncomfortable feeling will it settle down.

While adults aren't usually frustrated by the same kinds of situations that infants are, our reactions to frustration are pretty much the same as in our infant days. That is, we may fuss and holler and become overly preoccupied with whatever it is that is frustrating us, convincing ourselves that the situation is a major crisis and that it needs to be fixed *right now*!

The inner brat is the self-absorbed component of our minds that has roots in the infantile need for immediate gratification. We have since learned other skills for satisfying urges and coping with frustration, and we tend to rely on those other skills, mainly because they're more effective than kicking and screaming. But the more primitive responses are never erased or forgotten. They are still there, ready, under certain mental and environmental conditions, to emerge as inner-brat thoughts and behaviors.

Certain conditions encourage bratty thoughts, feelings, and behaviors, as discussed in chapter 11. For now, it is important to recognize that narcissistic characteristics are normal. They occur in everyone. They do differ from one person to another, however, in terms of when and how they are recognized and expressed. People who learn to tolerate frustration have less trouble with their inner brat than do those who make mountains out of molehills and keep saying to themselves, "I can't stand it!"

In addition to excessive self-absorption, narcissism also includes a sense of self-righteousness or entitlement. This attitude too originates in our infancy and early childhood. Young children's needs are not complex. They are satisfied with love and attention, sensory and mental stimulation, as well as food and shelter. Most parents can easily provide such amenities for their baby and can usually do so when the baby demands it. Thus, young children come to expect that they will receive whatever they desire, when they desire it.

For example, when a baby is bored, she might start fussing. Since most parents can't tolerate fussing for very long, they'll pick up the baby, bounce her, coo to her, or do something else to stimulate her; she stops fussing and everyone's happy. Another example is the toddler who wanders away from his mother, becomes frightened by the strangeness of his surroundings, and comes running back to her. It's not too difficult for the mother to scoop him up and provide reassurance. In general, babies and young children are easily appeased, and they learn to expect to be appeased immediately.

Me First

Some people never outgrow this expectation to be instantly appeased. You probably know some of them, or maybe you're one of them yourself.

These include people who become indignant when asked to wait their turn. An apocryphal story, attributed to a check-in clerk at the counter of a major airline, goes something like this: After a flight was canceled one busy morning, the passengers were asked to form a line in order to book another reservation. A well-dressed man walked up to the counter, trying to get the attention of the harried clerk just as she was about to take care of the next person in line. "I need to get on the next flight as soon as possible," he demanded, waving his old boarding pass. "Yes, sir," she replied. "If you'll just step to the back of the line, I'll check for you as soon as I can." The man then raised his voice a few decibels: "Do you know who I am?" he roared. At that point, the woman smiled pleasantly, picked up a telephone, and announced over the intercom for all to hear, "Airport security, please come to Gate 16. We have a passenger who has forgotten who he is." This story, as I said, may be apocryphal. But one thing is for sure: There are countless individuals, like the one depicted here, who expect to be waited on, who disregard others' needs, and who don't even recognize their own selfishness. The narcissistic, me-first approach is typical inner-brat expression.

As mentioned in chapter 5, societal influences, especially the media, have promoted the idea of speed and instant satisfaction as ideal. Nevertheless, most people know the difference between getting things done quickly and efficiently, on the one hand, and stepping on other people's toes, on the other. It's just that they sometimes act as if they don't.

"I'm the King of the World!"

This is the cry of exhilaration by the young hero in the movie *Titanic* as he rode the bow of the majestic ship. We all like to feel that sense of "It doesn't get any better than this" which occurs when we are consumed with our own elation. At such times it feels as if the world exists just for us, if only for the moment. For most people, such peak experiences occur only rarely. But those with a strong inner brat expect the world to revolve around them on a daily basis. Their wants and desires are urgent. Their work is more important than anyone else's. They might have made a mistake, but they expect you to "Give me a break." Nothing bad or even inconvenient should ever happen to them, their children, or even their pets. When they are ill or upset, everyone is supposed to cater to them.

It's not hard to see where such an attitude may have come from. Again, let's look back on childhood. Young children are very appealing. Parents and other adults like to watch them and exclaim over every accomplishment: Johnny's first step; Mary's first word; Timmy's first bowel movement in the toilet. Parents make major events out of such milestones. It is not surprising, therefore, that children assume the world revolves around them. In their own world, it does, and they expect it to continue that way.

But as they grow older, they face a rude awakening. They must learn to share. They must learn to wait. They must understand that they aren't always the center of the universe. This point is made quite clear when a baby brother or sister enters the picture, and it is further emphasized when they begin interacting with other children at school and on the playground. The road to learning how to share parents' attention can be a rocky one. Kids don't consult training manuals. They learn mostly by trial and error and by example.

If parents don't set limits through this learning period, children will continue to demand more and more and to expect their demands to be fulfilled immediately. In the extreme, parents can potentially raise little monsters. This was illustrated in an episode of the 1960s television show *The Twilight Zone* in which a six-year-old boy had mental powers that could destroy things and people just by willing it with his mind. After most of the people were gone, those remaining catered to his every whim, shuddering whenever he became the least bit upset, lest they also be banished to the cornfield.

We don't typically think of children as having that much power, but visit any supermarket on a Friday night, when many families shop for their weekly supply of groceries. There's a good chance that you'll see parents, tired from a busy week at work, give in to their youngsters' requests for various cereals, cookies, and other junk food, just to keep the kids quiet.

A behavior-modification training film opens with a scene of two little girls. One of them is licking a huge lollipop. The other asks her where she got it. "I got it for whining," she boasts. "What?" asks the other girl. "You see," says the first girl, "I asked my mom for a lollipop but she said 'no.' Then I asked her again, and she said 'no' again. So I started whining and whining, and she finally gave it to me." The mother of this girl, having given in just to keep her quiet, had unwittingly rewarded her for whining. Not only was it a poor choice for that particular situation, but it also increased the likelihood that the girl will whine again whenever she wants something. She doesn't know it, but her inner brat is gaining strength.

Brenda

Brenda was an adorable child. At age four she could read, play Bach minuets on her tiny violin, and stand on her head—not all at the same time, of course. She loved to perform for her parents and other relatives, who marveled at her accomplishments and lavished praise on her. When her little brother was born, that all changed. Brenda couldn't understand why an infant who couldn't even tie his own shoelaces could be so fascinating to adults. Her parents still listened to her read or play the violin, and they still watched while she tried to ride her two-wheeler, but they always seemed to have one eye on the baby. It was clear to Brenda that she was no longer the center of attention, but she was going to fix that. She'd make sure that people would notice her.

Brenda started to become more and more loud and demanding. If she didn't get noticed right away, she would pester people until they paid attention to her. Over the next few years, she earned the reputation of "show-off." No one argued that Brenda wasn't talented, because she was. However, she seemed to need to prove it too much. For example, she bragged about winning the school spelling bee. She made fun of kids who didn't know their multiplication tables. She pranced around her gymnastics class, doing backflips in front of children who were just mastering their balance. She didn't have any close friends, but her mother said that it was because she was gifted and that other people were probably intimidated by her many talents. She reassured Brenda that once she got to college, she'd meet more people like herself.

Later, in college, Brenda continued her attention-getting behavior. She couldn't understand why she didn't have any friends. After all, she was bright and entertaining; who *wouldn't* want to be associated with her? Lonely and depressed, she made an appointment with a psychologist at the counseling center. She went only for two sessions. Expecting that he'd be sympathetic and understanding, she poured her heart out to him. She told him how her parents paid more attention to her brother than to her and no matter how hard she tried, they never gave her the same amount of recognition. Her brother needed extra help in school with reading and math. When he got a B on his report card, her parents were thrilled. But when she got a B, they expressed disappointment, grumbling that she could do better.

The psychologist was not moved by her sad story. "So tell me," he asked. "What's the problem now?" "I'm depressed," she answered. "Everyone on campus seems to be so happy. They get invited to parties and other get-togethers. My phone hardly ever rings, and the only e-mail I get is for class announcements."

"From what you've told me," said the psychologist, "it's quite obvious that you're unhappy. But you seem to blame it mostly on your parents and other people. So far I haven't heard what you're trying to do to improve the situation." He showed no sympathy. Brenda rolled her eyes at him. "If I knew what to do to improve the situation," she seethed indignantly, "I wouldn't have needed to come here, would I?" With that, she announced that she was late for another appointment and would have to leave now.

Brenda did return for a second visit, mainly because her parents urged her to, but her heart wasn't in it. When the psychologist tried to get her to understand that she was being self-centered, she felt that he didn't care about her. She said to herself, "He's telling me to just get over it." In a sense, he was. Brenda's inner brat decided that being the center of attention was of paramount importance. She needed friends, and they were supposed to come to her, not the other way around. How could she expect herself to approach other people and take the risk of being rejected?

Brenda was raised to believe that being attractive and entertaining was enough. Early in her life, she didn't have to work too hard to get attention. She was one of those young children who are regarded as "terminally cute." However, cute goes only so far. As she got older, Brenda never learned to compromise or to show true sympathy for others. Although she was fun to be around, people didn't get the feeling that she truly cared about *them*. She was lonely because she had become too preoccupied with her own wants and desires.

How Did We Get So Bratty?

Fifty years ago, children did not talk back to their parents—not necessarily because they revered their elders but because they were intimidated by them. Today's children are not intimidated by much. To understand why, let's first look at their parents' generation, the baby boomers.

Baby boomers got their name from the post–World War II surge in population that occurred during a time of increasing economic stability and prosperity. Sociologists called it the "baby boom" because of its impact on society. New schools had to be built to accommodate the droves of incoming students. More teachers were hired. Playgrounds were built. Mothers stayed home to look after their children, but in contrast to previous generations, these mothers had washing machines, vacuum cleaners, and other labor-saving devices, which left them plenty of free time to spend with the children. Also in contrast to previous generations, many new families lived in communities at some distance from other relatives. For the first time in history, children became the focal point of the community. Priorities were no longer the needs of the extended family; instead, parents focused on the children.

Televisions made their way into homes during the 1950s. Some of the most popular programs were aimed at children. As television became a popular family activity, advertisers directed their messages to children, even going so far as to instruct them to tell their parents to buy them breakfast cereals, toys, sneakers, and other products. Never before had children had so much influence on their parents' decisions. It was no longer a matter of "get the kids what they need." It was now "get the kids what they want."

The baby-boom generation literally drove the advertising and entertainment industry. As the boomers went through various developmental stages, advertisers followed them closely, looking for trends and trying to anticipate their needs. From early childhood to middle age, the baby-boom generation became the central focus of the American economy. They were indulged first by their parents and, later, as they earned their own comfortable incomes, by themselves.

Childrearing and education became centered on children's feelings and self-esteem. During the 1950s, Dr. Benjamin Spock, a pediatrician, wrote what became the parents' bible on how to raise healthy and happy children. He told parents to treat children with respect and to consider their emotional as well as their physical needs. Unfortunately, many parents took this to mean backing off on discipline entirely. They focused too much on feelings, fearing that discipline might damage their children's self-confidence, initiative, and creativity.

In the 1970s, schools changed their curricula from spelling and reading drills to lessons that were supposedly more meaningful, but in reality, they were just more entertaining, because it was believed that boredom was toxic to children. The most important thing was to help children feel good about themselves and to have high self-esteem. In hindsight, we now know from research that high self-esteem alone does not improve school achievement. In fact, unrealistically high self-esteem stifles the urge to improve.

Traditional discipline in the schools was also challenged in the 1970s. Until that time, youngsters were expected to sit at their desks for several hours per day. There were always a few who would not or could not do so, and they were sent to the principal's office or given extra work to do. Some children received physical punishment. Child advocates of the 1970s spoke out against physical punishment and succeeded in outlawing it in most states. This change was generally a good thing, since research demonstrates that spanking does not teach a child right from wrong; it only deters behavior when the authority figure actively polices the situation.

But child advocates went too far when they recommended that the schools adapt to the child rather than requiring children to adapt to the school environment. For example, to accommodate youngsters who didn't sit still at their desks, schools experimented with open classrooms, where learning stations replaced desks and where several subjects were taught in a large space without walls separating the different areas. To the untrained eye, this environment looked quite disorganized, but experts of the time assured us that distractible children could learn more effectively in a less structured environment. Children seemed to enjoy this environment. They did not get into trouble for wandering around, because that was expected. They had the freedom to do just about anything they wanted to, and they didn't have to put up with the drudgery of homework. However, their learning and achievement did not improve. The open-classroom idea was a flop.

Summarizing thus far, excessive brattiness in our society emerged from circumstances under which the baby-boom generation grew up: Housing, education, manufacturing, entertainment, and advertising were all directed at making their lives more comfortable. With extended families no longer living close together, the children of the nuclear family, rather than the larger family as a whole, became the focus of attention. Baby boomers got the impression that the world revolved around them. And in their world, it did. The culture in which they grew up encouraged a narcissistic view of the world in which youngsters assumed that everything they did and thought was extraordinarily important and that they deserved to be catered to.

Of course, not all children grew up with such a sense of self-importance and entitlement. I'm referring to trends and statistics, to which there are always exceptions. Other influences, such as specific circumstances and individual personality traits and interactions, also affect how people view themselves and the world. But overall, the baby-boom generation was more self-centered than previous ones.

Self-centeredness is characteristic not only of the baby boomers. It has become entrenched in our culture. Author and social critic Tom Wolfe described the '70s as the "Me Decade." This was a time of encounter groups, self-discovery, and emphasis on personal experience. Self-gratification was paramount. "If it feels good, do it," we were encouraged, and if someone is offended by it, well, that's their problem. The divorce rate skyrocketed as people realized that they didn't feel "fulfilled" in their marriages and that they had to leave in order to "find themselves."

Books with titles such as *Looking Out for Number One* and *Pulling Your Own Strings* were best-sellers month after month. Books and magazine articles on self-improvement became the most popular form of reading material, and still remain so today. Although the subject areas have changed some—from personal fulfillment to achieving personal wealth, then to improved relationships, and most recently to spirituality—the emphasis continues to be on "me as the center of the universe." The "Me Decade" seems to be turning into the "Me Era."

The narcissistic theme is also evident in the proliferation of personal accounts of normal life events. For example, have you noticed how many people—especially celebrities—are writing about their childbirthing experiences, their hot flashes, their retirement, their fiftieth birthday, and other events as if they have discovered these experiences? As if no one else before has ever had such experiences? They also write about their childhood ordeals, their divorces, and their latest bout with addiction or disease, all assuming that their personal struggles are of major interest to the public. They go on television talk shows to draw attention to themselves, under the guise that they are trying to help others. Excuse me, but most of our great-grandmothers had babies, raised them, passed their fiftieth birthdays, and got through menopause and maybe even an epidemic or two without needing guidance from a popular television star or sports figure.

In his 1979 book, *The Culture of Narcissism*, the late social critic Christopher Lasch argued that America is in an "age of diminishing expectations." He was dismayed by the emphasis that society places on celebrity, charisma, and consumer goods. He noted that being admired and envied is valued more than being skilled. His paraphrase of an old maxim still rings true today: "Nothing succeeds like the appearance of success."[11] That is, it's not so important what you've accomplished but whether you've been noticed and admired.

We all like to believe that we are unique and special. Well, it is true that no two people, even identical twins, are exactly alike. Each of us is unique. But does that entitle us to special treatment? Years ago, the cartoon *Pogo* satirized this "uniqueness" phenomenon. One of the characters, "Pup Dog," was considered to be extremely valuable, because he was one of a kind. Ironically, this is what defines a mutt. In a sense, we're all mutts, each of us distinctive in our own way, but not necessarily deserving of special recognition because of it.

There's at least one person who disagrees. In Britain, a woman recently applied for a patent on herself, insisting that her application qualifies, because she meets the legal standard of "novel" and "useful." Here's what she has to say about it: "It has taken 30 years of hard labor for me to discover and invent myself, and now I wish to protect my invention from unauthorized exploitation."[12]

Technology: Have It Your Way

The invention of the VCR has transformed how we watch television. No longer are we at the mercy of the stations' schedules. We can tape and watch anything when *we* want. Furthermore, we can use the remote control to fast-forward whenever we choose not to watch a commercial or portion of a program. With the advent of the Internet, we can research, shop, and communicate at our convenience. We have become used to controlling when and how we receive information.

We also expect technology to meet our needs on other fronts. Space exploration, war equipment, and advances in medical procedures no longer amaze us. In fact, we have come to expect that technology should be available to solve all our problems. The media have perpetuated this expectation. Where else but in the movies could someone with a laptop computer save the world with a few quick keystrokes?

As technology becomes more advanced, we increasingly assume that we have more control over our lives than we actually do. Mistakes are not tolerated. Everything should work when we need it. Our sense of security and our arrogance about controlling things was shaken by the supposed Y2K bug, which threatened to shut down computers all over the world. As the year 1999 drew to a close, there was increased panic about potential disasters in air travel, basic utilities, and financial information. Every major company and government agency prepared for possible catastrophe. Fortunately, the year 2000 arrived without incident, and people around the world heaved a sigh of relief. Unfortunately, within a few months, this threat became a dim memory, and we are back to expecting technology to serve our own needs on our own time. Burger King's former popular slogan, "Have it your way," has extended to our daily lives.

In Your Face

People are more confrontational with each other these days. They shout more, and they listen less. Rudeness has become rampant. Police officers, teachers, and other traditional authority figures no longer have the respect they did fifty years ago.

Challenging authority is not new. But until this century, it was limited to outlaws and visionaries. Now it seems that everyone gets a kick out of bucking the system. It's seen as gutsy and sometimes heroic. Consider some of the songs that accompany modern television commercials: "Born to Be Wild" (Lucent Technology), "Bad to the Bone" (General Motors), and "Start Me Up" (Microsoft). These glorify individualism, disregard for tradition, and freedom from restraint.

We also see the glorification of adolescent rebellion in popular television shows. A few years ago, the defiant attitude of *Beavis and Butthead* was a favorite among adolescents. More recently, *South Park* gained popularity. Family sitcoms have also changed. In the 1950s, *Father Knows Best*, *The Donna Reed Show*, and *Leave It to Beaver* depicted intact families with clear authority figures. At the end of each show there was some lesson to be learned. While the families on these shows represented more the ideal than everyday reality, they did reflect the culture's respect for benevolent authority. Decades later, television parents are no longer portrayed as knowledgeable or authoritative. Instead, they serve as the foil for their wisecracking teenagers. Current script writers—many of them not too far out of adolescence themselves—characterize the parents as clueless or incompetent, while the children are clever and mischievous but adorable.

Adolescent-type rebelliousness isn't limited to adolescents, either. Middle-aged men who dress like their sons—in baggy T-shirts and baseball caps worn backwards—are not just making a fashion statement. They're communicating that not only do they still feel like kids at heart, but they also espouse antiauthoritarian values. They're "cool."

Childrearing in a Bratty Society

Today's parents tend to be more concerned with their children liking them than with what is ultimately best for their offspring. They want to be buddies more than disciplinarians. Recall that earlier in this chapter, I pointed out that narcissistic people feel easily wounded by rejection, by criticism, and even by indifference. That is why parents of today have difficulty setting limits and laying down the law. They can't bear the thought of their children being upset with them. These are the parents who tell their children, "You're grounded for a week!" but back down, sometimes within a matter of an hour or two. Children learn not to take such threats seriously. In my work with children, some have confided to me that they assume most punishments won't be enforced, so it's worth taking a chance on getting away with something they shouldn't do.

Parents of today tend to view their children as extensions of themselves. How else could we explain parents' tantrums and rages on sports fields where their children are playing? It's not unusual to hear mothers and fathers berate the game officials, the coaches, and the other players when they believe that their own child has been treated unfairly. Sometimes the results can be fatal. In July 2000, one father beat another father to death in Massachusetts at an ice-hockey rink where their children were practicing. Apparently, he didn't like the way his son was being treated by the other man.

When parents view their children as extensions of themselves, it is very important to them that the children score lofty achievements, that they don't get their feelings hurt, and that they are respected by their peers. In an effort to protect their children from hurt feelings, parents side with them against authority. Fifty years ago, if a child got into trouble at school, he was punished first at school and again when he got home. Nowadays, parents are more likely to seek "justice" by hiring an attorney and suing the school. Consider the recent case of a high school valedictorian in Oregon who was stripped of her honor after she decided to take a shower in the boys' locker room. She sued the school but lost. Her mother was disappointed with the decision, saying nonchalantly that her eighteen-year-old daughter is "spontaneous and fun, and some people don't like that."

This girl and others whose parents defend their foolish actions learn not only that their own agendas are more important than are those of their community but also that it is quite acceptable to show contempt for authority even when you are clearly in the wrong. Such views encourage development of an inner brat.

It is evident that the generation of people who were raised to assume that they are the center of the universe now project their own needs onto their children, such that they regard their children as an extension of themselves. Because they are not consistent in discipline and because the consequences are unpredictable, their children do not take them all that seriously and can usually get away with misbehavior and disrespect.

In *The Sibling Society*, Robert Bly describes the current adult generation as adolescent "half-adults" who behave like jealous siblings, each demanding personal gratification while scorning mutual responsibility and natural authority. Society's heroes are not wise, learned adults but sports figures and rock stars. Bly laments that the commercialization of life has trivialized it to the point where we have all become alienated and where our lives have become devoid of meaning.[13]

While I don't hold such a gloomy view of society, it is apparent that the more self-absorbed we become, the less happy we are. The incidence of depression has more than doubled over the past two decades. We know more about how the mind works, but we have not made much progress in controlling our thoughts and behaviors. The inner brat has been nurtured and encouraged by a distorted view of our place in the world. It's time to see things in perspective and get that brat under control. In the next two chapters, you will confront your own inner brat. You'll learn to recognize it and learn its tricks. It's more complex than you think but not as powerful as it seems.

7

How Strong Is Your Inner Brat?

I don't know anyone who *doesn't* have an inner brat. We all have moments when we succumb to impulsive desires, to anger that gets out of control. Nobody is completely sensible, selfless, and restrained. However, some people's inner brat can become an outer brat with very little provocation. The following short quiz will help you determine your "Brat quotient." Answer the questions as you *usually* behave or could see yourself behaving. Scoring instructions are at the end of the quiz.

1. You have been waiting on hold for more than five minutes. You
   a. Hang up the telephone and decide to try again later.
   b. Open your mail, read a magazine, or find something to keep you occupied.
   c. Fuss and fume, such that when the person finally answers, you are considerably less than cordial.

2. While driving, you are stopped by a police officer who states that you were speeding. You

    a. Keep quiet and don't say anything.

    b. Ask him politely how he arrived at his conclusion.

    c. Argue vehemently that you couldn't have been speeding and, as he walks away, yell, "I'll see you in court!"

3. You've been sticking to your diet all week. Now you're at the dessert buffet. You

    a. Walk away from it without looking back.

    b. Put a small morsel on your plate and eat one or two bites.

    c. Take a small piece of cake and come back six more times for another small piece.

4. You learn that your spouse shared with a friend something that you had assumed would be confidential. You

    a. Shrug it off and forget about it.

    b. Civilly discuss your concerns with your spouse.

    c. Lose your temper and threaten never to share your private thoughts again.

5. You are committed in your relationship, but you find yourself attracted to someone else at work. You

    a. Decide to try to forget about the attraction and not even think about it.

    b. Acknowledge your feelings but decide that acting on them could create unnecessary complications in your life.

    c. Start flirting, knowing that your significant other will probably never find out

6. Your mother didn't call you on your birthday. You feel hurt. You

    a. Say nothing to her and act as if you weren't hurt.

    b. Tell her you were disappointed.

    c. Say nothing to her but act cool and distant for several weeks or months.

7. Your closet is a mess. Your clothes are so jammed together that everything you choose to wear needs ironing. You

    a. Promise yourself that *for sure* this weekend you'll sort every-thing out and get rid of items that you haven't worn in two years.

    b. Pick out a half-dozen items that you haven't worn and pack them to give away.

    c. Frantically tear a bunch of clothes off the hangers and throw them into a pile in the middle of the floor so that you have more room.

8. You've found an interesting but complicated recipe in a magazine. You spend most of the day shopping for ingredients and preparing the meal. When you serve it to your family, it's not the hit that you expected. You

    a. Wonder what you did wrong.

    b. Ask them for specific suggestions for improvement.

    c. Vow never to try new recipes again.

9. At one of your favorite restaurants, the service is unusually slow. You

   a. Sit patiently, looking at your watch every few minutes.

   (b.) Find the manager and quietly ask what the problem is.

   c. Get up and loudly announce that you're leaving, making sure that everyone in the restaurant knows why.

10. At your annual performance evaluation at work, your boss makes some statements that you believe are inaccurate. You

   a. Say nothing, hoping that no one else will read your evaluation.

   (b.) Allow the boss to finish, then state specifically what you disagree with, and ask for that to be noted on the evaluation form.

   c. Threaten to sue your boss and the company.

11. You decide to take up a new sport like golf or tennis. You find that it's a lot harder than it looks. You

   a. Buy expensive clothing and equipment so that you can feel more professional.

   (b.) Sign up for a series of lessons.

   c. Quit and declare that sports are a waste of time.

12. You're riding in the car with your teenager, who just got his learner's permit. He lurches ahead too fast and brakes too abruptly. You

   a. Say nothing, figuring that he will eventually get the hang of it.

   (b.) Suggest that he apply his foot more gradually to the gas pedal and brake.

   c. Gasp and brace yourself every time he brakes, complaining that he's going to kill you both if he keeps driving that way.

13. You're trying to concentrate on a difficult reading assignment in the library. Two people at the next table are whispering loudly and laughing. You've already asked them once to keep it down. Now you
    a. Glare at them, hoping to stare them down so that they'll feel intimidated and stop.
    b. Get up and find another table to work at.
    c. Find the librarian and demand that she make them leave.

14. After the breakup of your last relationship, you learn that your ex is spreading untrue gossip about you. You
    a. Ignore the gossip, hoping it will go away.
    b. Call your ex and request that the gossip stop.
    c. Retaliate by spreading false rumors about your ex.
    d. Tell people it's untrue.

15. You've abstained from cigarettes, junk food, or alcohol for three days. Suddenly you get a craving. You
    a. Give up. It's too hard to resist.
    b. Figure out a way to hold out for the rest of the day.
    c. Convince yourself that you'll just take a break for a while and begin abstaining again next week.

16. You have been putting off a major task at work, and the deadline is looming. You
    a. Call in sick, hoping that the boss might be sympathetic and give you an extension.
    b. Spend some time *today* working on the task.
    c. Blame co-workers for not giving you the information you need.

2

Check your answers. If you have a lot of "*a*" responses, you are passive and allow things to happen to you. You may have a rigid, all-or-nothing approach to life, and you may also harbor resentment, which could trigger inner-brat thoughts and behaviors.

12 If you have a lot of "*b*" responses, you probably exercise rational control much of the time. Congratulations.

2 If you have many "*c*" answers, you are easily frustrated and take it out on others. Consequently, your inner brat probably gets you into a lot of trouble.

If you have fewer "*b*" responses than "*a*" and "*c*" combined, your inner brat can use some work. In the next few chapters, you will find useful techniques to help you gain control.

This quiz is not a scientific study. There are no statistics on what is "normal" as far as the inner brat is concerned. The questions illustrate typical situations in which people find themselves. For example, in the circumstances described in questions 1 and 9, we would probably feel annoyed. We could choose to do nothing, express rage (compliments of our inner brat), or think of a rational solution that will get results.

In questions 3 and 11, we are addressing self-discipline. If we give up or make excuses, our inner brat is at work. On the other hand, if we take charge of the situation we feel more effective and competent.

Questions 12 and 14 involve how we deal with other people when we are upset with them. The choices are to try to ignore our feelings, to express outrage, or to discuss things rationally. The rational approach always leaves us feeling less frustrated than do the other two courses of action.

If you recognize within yourself a pattern of avoiding or overreacting, of lacking self-discipline, or of losing your temper, then your inner brat has a grip on you.

In the next chapter you will become familiar with the many ways that the inner brat manifests itself. You might be surprised by its versatility.

8

The Many Personae of the Inner Brat

The inner brat has many faces. While it basically reflects self-centered, impulsive forces within us, it can manifest itself in a number of different ways. Think of your inner brat as a clever actor who can play many roles. As pointed out earlier in the brief descriptions of Eric Berne's theory of Child, Parent, and Adult ego states, you, as a person, already play many roles throughout the day.

For example, at work you probably behave in a more professional manner than when playing with children. Your conduct in the dentist's chair is different from that at the football stadium. You adopt different roles to fit various situations. These roles are not necessarily artificial or insincere; they are based on your previous experiences in specific circumstances. They often occur without your thinking about it, even when switching from one role to another. Sometimes the results are amusing. I'm reminded of a time when I was in the waiting room of the veterinary clinic with my dog. Another pet owner and I began to chat in tones that one might consider casual conversation. When my dog suddenly sat up alert and turned her head toward the door, the other pet owner, a large man in a business suit, addressed my dog in a singsong voice that's usually observed in mothers talking to their babies: "What's the matter?" he cooed. "Puppy hear a noisy-woisy?" Without realizing it, this man had shifted roles from conventional adult chitchat to squeaky baby talk. Most likely that's how he talked to his own pets.

Not all role-switching is unconscious. You often are aware of changing your tone or manner. If you've ever played with a rambunctious child, you probably know what I mean. Suppose you're tossing a ball back and forth indoors and having so much fun that both of you start to get silly. Perhaps you throw the ball a little harder or bounce it off a chair. With this kind of encouragement, the child will probably carry the silliness to an extreme, perhaps hitting you a little too hard with the ball or accidentally breaking something. In order to bring the situation under control, you must change your role from playful companion to stern adult. You do this consciously with the goal of achieving a specific result.

The inner brat also switches roles to fit different situations. It too uses both conscious and unconscious strategies. But its goals are always limited to immediate gratification or immediate relief. Remember, your inner brat wants what it wants, when it wants it, and will do whatever it takes, without regard for the consequences. If one strategy doesn't work, it will try another. It is confrontational at some times and manipulative at others.

In the following section are some examples of the roles that your inner brat might assume. While your inner brat won't necessarily display all of these characteristics, it probably has two or three preferred roles.

From the descriptions, see if you can identify which are the favorites of your inner brat.

The Nag

Think of this inner brat as a nagging voice inside you. The voice nags and pesters, drowning out other voices that try to convince you to be reasonable. For example, think back to the last holiday season. Remember all those times you told yourself you weren't going to overeat but did so anyway? That was your inner brat at work. While looking at all the food and drink, it kept nagging you, "I want it . . . I must have it . . . You shouldn't deprive me." The brat drowns out the other voices in your head, the voices that caution you to use reason. Your reasonable voice may say, "You've just had a huge dinner and you know you're not hungry," but the inner brat shouts over this voice, perhaps claiming that the chocolate mousse looks delicious and "I just absolutely must have some!"

If your inner brat tends to nag, you will find yourself in frequent conflict with urges and desires. Part of you will want something badly while another part will tell you why it's unreasonable or unnecessary. The Nag inner brat is often present at times when you are trying to reform bad habits, especially when you are trying to *refrain* from something, such as food, cigarettes, or alcohol.

The Nag is also operative when you feel a strong sexual attraction to someone. The persistent thoughts and obsessions are consistent with the nagging quality of this inner brat. I'm not referring here to that heavenly feeling we call infatuation, where we feel lighthearted and in love. In this case, I'm speaking of those thoughts and feelings that accompany persistent lust, especially illicit lust. People who engage in extramarital affairs often have such feelings. Even though they know that adultery is wrong, they continue to indulge their urges. Their Nag inner brats persist in tempting them with forbidden desire.

The Rationalizer

If you don't pay attention to your inner brat's nagging, it may change its tactics. It assumes the role of a reasonable voice, but beware. This is not reason; it's rationalization and manipulation. This inner brat may try to tell you that you can eat all you want and just exercise it off tomorrow. It can persuade you to take just a tiny piece of cake, then another tiny piece, and so on, until you've devoured the whole thing. It can convince you that it's OK to buy all those new clothes even though the credit card is almost maxed out, because, after all, they're on sale. The inner brat wants a cigarette, but instead of coming right out and begging, it convinces you that you just need this last one to calm down. You spend long lunches with an attractive co-worker and share confidences that you wouldn't even tell your best friend, but according to your Rationalizer inner brat, that is justified because your own spouse shows so little interest in you.

The Rationalizer inner brat is sometimes hard to detect, because it uses logic. However, if you examine the initial premise from which the logic flows, you will notice a pattern. Almost always you'll find that the initial premise is "What I want is OK because..." or some variation thereof. Furthermore, the logic ignores contradictory information, such as the negative consequences of self-indulgence.

The Rationalizer inner brat uses its tactics to justify satisfying your cravings or urges. And it also comes into play when you refuse to acknowledge that you've offended or hurt someone.

Linda, a woman in her mid-thirties, has a habit of insulting and embarrassing people. She might say to a co-worker, "Where did you get that awful haircut?" or "How can you be so stupid!" Most of the time, people try to ignore Linda, but occasionally someone confronts her on her rudeness. Linda just shrugs it off. "You know I'm just kidding," she protests. "You're just way too sensitive." Her inner brat will never admit that she has overstepped the bounds of civility. She rationalizes her behavior in terms of the other person's sensitivity rather than her own rudeness.

The Eruptor

This inner brat has very little tolerance for frustration and demands that the world conform to its view. When things don't turn out as expected, it reacts with a vengeance. Not only is the Eruptor's overreaction draining, but it can be quite counterproductive as well. Here's an example: Alice was waiting for a repairman to come to her house to fix the washing machine. She had taken the morning off work, because she was told that he would be there before noon. When he wasn't there at eleven o'clock, she called the appliance store. They said that he was running late and that he had just left to pick up the part. He would be there after lunch. "After lunch!" Alice exclaimed. "I'm not waiting until after lunch! I have responsibilities, too, you know. Why didn't he call?" "I'm sorry, ma'am," said the voice on the other end of the line. "I don't know why he didn't call. But he can be there this afternoon, or we can reschedule." Alice was enraged. Her inner brat was in full control. "Never mind!" she exclaimed. "I'll call some-one else!" Now Alice's brat was satisfied. It had won the battle. But what had Alice won? She had to find another appliance repairman and had to use the laundromat for a week. That was an inconvenient price to pay for giving in to her inner brat.

People with a strong Eruptor inner brat are often said to be hotheaded or short-tempered. It doesn't take much to get them angry. The Eruptor inner brat is combative, always needing to prove a point, always needing to "win." To give in is considered weak.

The Smolderer

The inner brat doesn't always rage when it gets mad. Sometimes it does a slow burn, amassing energy for its anger by provoking other people. Jenny didn't get a valentine gift, or even a card, from her husband. She was disappointed. Her inner brat was furious. But this time it didn't rage—it seethed. "Obviously, you don't love me," she told her husband, "because if you did, you would have thought at least to buy me a card." Jenny didn't leave it at that. For the next several days she pointed out numerous other examples of her husband's thoughtlessness. He left his shoes in the middle of the floor; he parked his car directly behind hers in the driveway, knowing full well that she might have to leave for work before he did; he didn't notice that the laundry needed to be folded. Each time Jenny noticed such carelessness, she drew it to his attention, using a voice so sarcastic that he could feel his skin crawl. Finally, he couldn't take it anymore and yelled at her, telling her that she could just take her complaining to her mother's house and stay there. This was all Jenny needed.

Now she had another confirmation of her husband's rejection. The irony of it was that she couldn't understand why he felt so hostile toward her.

The Smolderer inner brat presents itself as a victim. It feels sorry for itself. It pouts and sulks, sometimes for days or weeks on end, reliving unpleasant episodes over and over again. It magnifies and dwells on the negative. If your inner brat tends to smolder, you may find yourself feeling down or depressed. You may feel that other people avoid you or don't respect you. How else should they treat you when all they see in you is negativity?

The Whiner

The Whiner inner brat finds fault with almost everything. It believes that it should never be the slightest bit inconvenienced. Like the Smolderer, it feels very much the victim, but it is much more vocal than the Smolderer. Like the Eruptor, it does not tolerate frustration. However, it does not explode—it merely complains. It gripes about big things, like losing money in the stock market or missing a job interview because you had forgotten to write it down in your calendar. It also whines about minor things, like waiting in line or getting stuck in traffic. The Whiner brat doesn't differentiate between major and minor inconveniences. Any type of disturbance is considered an agonizing catastrophe.

Like all inner brats, the Whiner doesn't acknowledge any responsibility for its circumstances. It feels constantly victimized. It laments its predicament but never looks for solutions. It is more interested in blaming other people or circumstances. The Whiner wants things corrected immediately but is not willing to exert effort toward making corrections happen. People with a strong Whiner inner brat are known as chronic complainers or "poor sports."

Stuart's inner brat is a whiner. He claims that he should have won the club's tennis championship last year, but his games were always scheduled during bad weather. Besides, his chief opponent used an oversize racquet, which provided an unfair advantage. Stuart is ready to tell anyone who's willing to listen about the unfairness of it all.

Miriam has interviewed for many jobs but has not yet been offered a position. She is positive that her lack of success is due to employers hiring minority applicants to fill racial quotas. She knows she can do a better job than anyone, but no employer is willing to give her a chance.

Russ makes sure to tell each first date that it was his ex-wife and her constant criticism that caused the breakup of his marriage. He spends a full hour describing how he suffered in her presence. Needless to say, he rarely gets a second date.

If you find yourself dissatisfied a great deal of the time, complaining excessively, finding fault with others, or making excuses, you probably have a strong Whiner inner brat. This is especially true if you don't take steps to make positive changes.

The Exhibitionist

The Exhibitionist inner brat needs to be noticed and admired. It will dominate conversations, dramatize minor situations, and command attention whenever and wherever possible. This inner brat does not realize that it is alienating everyone else, because it's too busy with its own self-importance. It talks but doesn't listen.

Glen fancies himself the life of the party. He loves an audience for his inane and sometimes crude jokes. When people snicker politely so as not to embarrass him, he mistakes such a reaction as endorsement of his behavior and continues on and on. If people try to change the subject, Glen talks louder, sometimes grabbing their arm to hold their attention.

Not all Exhibitionist inner brats are as obvious as Glen's. Veronica's inner brat is exhibitionistic but more subtly so. Whenever she hears bad news, she is the first to broadcast it. It may be news of someone's divorce or illness or a warning of a bad snowstorm. Veronica adds dramatic details far beyond those necessary. It is as if her inner brat is announcing, "Look at me! Remember, I'm the one who told you first!"

The Exhibitionist inner brat reflects one's narcissistic need for attention and admiration. People with this manifestation of the inner brat often feel deep down inside that they have little to offer in terms of their own talents or accomplishments, so they rely on shock and other attention-getting devices.

The Martyr

Like the Exhibitionist inner brat, the Martyr inner brat also wants to be noticed, but in a more focused way. The Martyr makes sacrifices and wants everyone to notice. No one suffers more than this inner brat. It dwells on all it has done for other people and on how little appreciation it gets in return. If you have a Martyr inner brat you probably become resentful when you don't get the recognition that you feel you deserve for your efforts.

Cathy has a strong Martyr inner brat. A self-acknowledged "neat freak," she knocks herself out cleaning and decorating her house. Like her mother before her, she wants her home to be immaculate and magazine-perfect. Unfortunately, her husband and children don't share her concern for order and neatness. It does not upset them to see a dirty plate on the counter or a wet towel on the bathroom floor. But these things drive Cathy mad. Her inner brat believes that her family deliberately refuses to put things away just to annoy her. "Can't you see I've worked so hard to make this place livable?" she hollers when she sees things out of place. Cathy feels unappreciated and lets everyone know it.

Not all Martyr inner brats are so vocal. Some individuals have a Martyr/Smolderer combination. This blend can be unnerving to other people. The Martyr/Smolderer makes its sacrifices quietly. It doesn't draw attention to itself directly, but it still wants other people to notice the ordeals it's suffered. And when they don't, the inner brat gets very quiet, but it's an icy quiet. For example, if Cathy's inner brat were more the quiet type, instead of yelling at her children when they left their coats on the back of a chair, she'd put away the coats and not say anything. However, she'd be distant for the rest of the evening. If someone were to ask her, "What's wrong?" she'd reply, "Nothing. Nothing at all," leaving everyone wondering what they had done to upset her.

The Bully

Like the Exhibitionist inner brat, the Bully likes to be the center of attention. But this inner brat is more concerned with having power and making sure that no one is going to tell it what to do. People with a strong Bully inner brat are aggressive and insensitive. An example of someone with a strong Bully inner brat is the abusive spouse. Some abusive spouses are women, but most are men. Furthermore, not all abusive spouses resort to physical aggression. In fact, most of them bully others verbally, through intimidation and threats. Charles is described as a take-charge person at work. A troubleshooter for the company's computer system, he always seems to know what to do when there's a problem. He works alone and is totally focused on his task. Some of his co-workers describe him as a perfectionist, but when one is dealing with pesky software problems, that's an asset. At home, his perfectionism extends to his expectations for his wife and children. "I work hard all day," he declares, "so when I come home I need to relax. I don't like to hear the kids fighting. I don't like to see mess and clutter. My job is to bring home a paycheck to support a nice home. My wife's job is to make sure that the home stays nice and that nothing is out of place." Charles doesn't like anything to interfere with his wife's primary job. That's why he listens in on her phone calls, doesn't allow her to go out with friends, and makes sure that the housework follows a schedule. If his wife challenges him, he threatens her by claiming that with his connections, he could have her declared an unfit mother and she would never see her children again. Charles does not think of his behavior as bullying. He claims to be a religious man who just wants what's right for his family. He admits that he hit his wife only once, early in their marriage, but she had "asked for it" with her defiant attitude. *challenges*

Charles's inner brat thrives on power. At work, where no one challenges him, his inner brat does not show itself readily. At home, his wife doesn't challenge him much either, but she does sneak behind his back, calling friends when she thinks he's not listening or lying that she's going to the grocery store when in fact she visits her sister. When Charles finds out about these deceptions, his inner brat emerges. This Bully inner brat is not to be outdone. It gets its revenge through intimidation and retaliation.

Normal or Abnormal?

Keep in mind that the inner-brat personalities portrayed here are not the same as emotional illnesses or criminal behavior. The inner brat may, in fact, be a component of emotional or criminal disturbance, but it does not entirely explain the extremes of suicidal depression, violent crime, serious distortion of reality, chronic alcoholism, and so on. These conditions are a product of a complex, multilayered mix of factors, which include not only personality traits and situational factors but also sociocultural and sometimes biological determinants.

The inner-brat personalities are merely a convenient way of describing how people deal with situations that are difficult or unpleasant. They are not diagnostic of any mental illness or condition. For the purposes of this book, I am referring to inner-brat characteristics of average people who, for the most part, function adequately in their lives but who periodically do or say things that they later regret.

Our Own Inner Brats Are Not Obvious to Us

In general, it's easier to spot the inner brat in someone else than in yourself. Whenever I lecture on this subject, as I describe various inner-brat personalities, I notice people in the audience affectionately poking their spouses or companions when they recognize a familiar description. These pokes are accompanied by glances and whispers that communicate, "See, that's you. I told you so."

Other people's shortcomings are always more obvious than your own. As I pointed out in chapter 3, you are more apt to attribute permanent character traits to someone else's negative behavior, while your own is excused as a temporary divergence. This tendency also extends to those you are close with. If you have children, you probably don't call them brats. When they misbehave, you attribute it to their fatigue, playful boisterousness, or other temporary physical or emotional states.

When your own child acts up, you say he is simply a little out of control. But if the neighbor's child acts the same way, you are more likely to attribute brat status to him, especially if you've seen him behave this way before.

Does this imply that you can't readily identify your own inner brat? No, but it does imply that unless you learn to do so, you will continue to blame other people and situations for whatever goes wrong in your life. Furthermore, because you won't feel in control of your life, you'll be chronically unhappy.

How the Inner Brat Transforms Itself

As I mentioned earlier, your inner brat, like most people's, probably changes its behavior from one situation to the next. You may or may not be aware that the changes are taking place. But whatever form your inner brat takes, you know it's there because of a nagging feeling of dissatisfaction that won't go away. You might try to do something to lessen that dissatisfaction, but if it doesn't disappear, it's because you inner brat is changing tactics.

Leonard is a forty-seven-year-old manager at a car dealership who is in charge of eight sales associates. When cars are selling well, Leonard is rewarded with bonuses, but when sales are down, he is called to explain why. The last time Leonard had to meet with the dealership owner, he prepared his reasons: "You know we've been having a lot of bad weather, Mr. Doyle. People just aren't coming in to the showroom. Even the discounts and rebates aren't luring them in." Mr. Doyle, the owner, countered with, "That's not what I observed. We've had only five fewer test drives this quarter than during the previous three months." Leonard replied, "I can't control everything around here. Jerry, Hank, and the other salesmen just aren't pushing the cars strongly enough. What do you expect me to do— barge in on their conversations with customers and embarrass them? How can you blame me when I don't even meet with the customers?" He stormed out of Mr. Doyle's office.

Later that evening at home, Leonard complained that his dinner was overcooked and that his wife had once again forgotten to pick up his dry cleaning. He isolated himself in the basement with an old television set and a bottle of gin and smoked one cigarette after another until 1 A.M. By then he was numb. Nothing had been solved. In fact, the next day, looking back on his behavior, Leonard could not believe that he had been so unpleasant.

Let's review how Leonard's inner brat caused havoc for him that day. First, when Mr. Doyle called him in to his office, Leonard tried to justify the slow sales for the previous three months. This was his Rationalizer inner brat, making excuses. When this didn't work, his inner brat turned into a Whiner, complaining that he was a victim of circumstances over which he had little or no control. As tension built inside him, his Eruptor inner brat took over. Later that night, his petty bickering with his wife reflected a Smolderer inner brat. Finally, his overindulgence in tobacco and alcohol was the product of the Nag, the inner-brat persona that just has to have what it wants and has to have it now.

Most people don't display so many inner-brat personalities within the span of a few hours. Leonard is not a real person but rather a composite of many people I have known, people whose inner brats make them unhappy with themselves and with others. Leonard illustrates how one's inner brat can transform itself.

Each transformation may be viewed as the inner brat's attempt to avoid discomfort or to seek satisfaction. But as you can see, it is not usually successful. It remains upset, disappointed, angry, or resentful until you and your conscious, rational mind take charge.

Your Own Personality and the Inner Brat

You've now become familiar with the various inner-brat personalities and may have identified your own inner brat. People's inner brats differ because their own basic personality traits differ. We saw earlier in this book how Craig, the extrovert, reacted to being confined to his home during a snowstorm. He became stir-crazy and eager to get out among people. On the other hand, I speculated that Trudy, the shy introvert, would not be nearly as uncomfortable in such a situation.

To illustrate how basic personality traits partially determine the way in which a person's inner brat expresses itself, let's consider extroverts and introverts. Extroverts, such as Craig, love to be around people. Their mental energies are directed externally toward people and events. Their attention is tuned to what's going on in the world around them. They are usually talkative and expressive. Introverts, like Trudy, on the other hand, are more tuned internally to their own thoughts and feelings. They are thoughtful and reflective and usually speak only when there's something important to say. (Keep in mind that not all extroverts have great social skills and that not all introverts are shy. The extroversion/introversion distinction refers to whether a person pays attention more to external or internal [mental] events.)

With this difference in mind, consider how an extrovert's inner brat might operate. Given that extroverts are directed outward, their inner brats will also tend to be directed outward. Loud, expressive inner brats, such as the Eruptor, the Exhibitionist, or the Bully are found more commonly with extroverted people than with the quieter introverts. Of course, not all extroverts have temper tantrums, nor do they all monopolize conversations, nor are they all bullies. But when their inner brats are in control, they often assume a loud expressive form, particularly when the situation is one of interpersonal conflict.

Alternatively, an introverted person's inner brat is usually expressed more internally in the form of brooding, grumbling, and self-pity. The Martyr and the Smolderer inner brats are more common among introverts. This again is not an ironclad rule. (Nothing is when it comes to the complex workings of the mind.) Some people with a strong Martyr inner brat are quite outgoing, and some people with a Bully inner brat are loners. But in general, the inner brat that appears first is the one which corresponds with one's personality style. If that doesn't get results, the inner brat can transform itself. Thus, while an introvert's inner brat might first appear as an internalizing Smolderer, it can very easily transform itself into an externalizing Eruptor.

Introversion and extroversion are only one dimension, albeit a major one, by which personality is described or measured. Other traits include independence, aggressiveness, and perfectionism. It is beyond the scope of this book to delineate all personality traits. Experts don't even agree on what constitutes personality and how personality traits are measured or described. Just keep in mind that your inner brat is influenced by the totality of characteristics that make up your unique personality.

Remember, your inner brat is not separate from you. I have been referring to it as if it is an entity unto itself, but that is only for the sake of convenience. The inner brat represents primitive thoughts, feelings, and behaviors, both conscious and unconscious, from infancy and early childhood. It is part of you, integrated into your personality. Your inner brat's personality reflects features of your general personality.

Personality style influences the inner brat most often in situations where there is interpersonal conflict, such as when you are angry at another person, when you feel jealous or envious, or when you feel ignored or rejected by someone. These feelings are communicated in some way through your behavior. Even when you don't speak up, your feelings are communicated. You may recall in chapter 2 the description of Sara, the store manager who was angry at her district supervisor but didn't tell her directly. Instead, Sara communicated via cold silence. The district supervisor interpreted Sara's behavior as a poor attitude. You may also recall that the situation remained unresolved. Sara's inner brat certainly expressed her unhappiness, but Sara stayed miserable because she communicated only that she was angry, not that she was interested in solving the problem.

In this chapter, you've seen how the inner-brat personae differ from one another. In the next chapter, you'll learn the ways in which they're similar.

9

Common Characteristics and Problems among the Various Brat Personae

In the last chapter, you learned about the different ways the inner brat can reveal itself. Most people's inner brats "morph" regularly from one persona to another. This is because if one strategy doesn't work, the inner brat tries another, and another, and so on until it achieves its goal. It manipulates you in any way it can.

In this chapter, you will see not the differences among inner brats but their similarities. As noted before, all inner brats have similar goals: to maximize pleasure and to minimize pain. They do this without regard for the consequences. That is why you often regret having said or done something that was initiated by your inner brat.

Inner brats also typically have a sense of entitlement, as described earlier. The inner brat represents the narcissistic demands that originated in your infancy and early childhood. As a young child, you probably exhibited bratty behavior quite often. If your parents did their job well, you learned less obnoxious ways of getting what you wanted. Nevertheless, some remnants of this sense of entitlement remain.

Another common characteristic among inner brats is that they communicate their wishes, demands, and complaints via bodily sensations as well as through language. You are probably familiar with the bodily tension you feel just prior to giving in to your inner brat. If you listen closely, you will also notice that your inner brat "talks" to you.

Brat "Morphing": Ryan

Let's first review the process of how an inner brat changes its tactics or "morphs" from one persona to another. This shifting results from experience and learning. Your inner brat has probably adopted two or three favorite tactics based on which ones have worked the best for you in the past. For example, if your Nag inner brat usually gets what it wants, then that becomes one of your preferred strategies. But the Nag may not always be successful, especially if you tend to feel guilty about indulging your impulses. In that case, your inner brat might morph into the Rationalizer, presenting supposedly logical reasons for following your urges.

We often see such "brat morphing" in children's behavior. Consider this scene between eight-year-old Ryan and his mother: One morning just before school, Ryan cheerfully asked his mother if he could take his pet rabbit to school. Not being sure about the school policy on bringing pets, Ryan's mother said, "Not today, buddy. I don't know whether it's allowed." Ryan tried to convince his mother that it was OK, but she didn't give in. "I'll find out later," she assured him. "But now you'd better hurry, or you'll miss the bus." Ryan didn't like her answer.

"Why can't I? It's *my* rabbit," he argued. "You told me it was my pet and that I have to take care of it. Well, I have been taking care of it. I feed it, I usually clean the cage, and I play with it all the time. So if I want to take it to school, I should be able to." By now, his mother was getting impatient and annoyed. "I said no!" she snapped back. Now Ryan was desperate. He was running out of time. He *needed* to take that rabbit to school. He'd promised his friends he was going to bring it, and if he didn't show up with it, his friends would think he was a liar. Ryan ran to his room and slammed the door. He threw himself on the bed, sobbing, making sure that it was loud enough for his mother to hear. Predictably, she entered his room and tried to reason with him, but he'd have none of that. He needed that rabbit. He started to hyperventilate, which always made his mother panic a little. "All right," she sighed. "You dry your eyes and get ready for the bus. I'll call the school and bring your rabbit a little later." Abruptly Ryan stopped crying. He had gotten what he wanted. He didn't thank his mother. He just said, "OK," in a half-sobbing voice, reluctantly agreeing with the compromise. To himself he thought smugly, "It worked again."

Fast-forward twenty years. For the most part, Ryan is fairly well-adjusted. He has a secure job with a promising future. He is married with one child. Money is a little tight, but the bills get paid. One of Ryan's dreams is to drive a little red sports car, but he knows it's not practical right now. Nevertheless, his inner brat nags him daily about it. Just like when he was a little boy and *needed* to take that rabbit to school, he now *needs* this little car. Of course, he knows he doesn't really need it, but sometimes it feels as if he can't wait until he's forty. He wants it now.

Ryan's inner brat tries the nagging routine, but he is far too practical to give in to that. So, just as he did previously as a young boy with his mother, his inner brat tries rationalizing. It tries to convince him that a sports car is an investment, that it will hold its value rather than depreciate like an ordinary car. It reminds him that it would be a good opportunity for him to show his son how to take care of something valuable. The inner brat is gaining ground, but it hasn't won yet. After a few weeks, Ryan becomes obsessed with buying a sports car. He can't sleep. His inner brat is figuratively screaming at him. He sometimes wakes up hyperventilating. What is happening to him internally is similar to his sobbing episode twenty years earlier. Just as his mother gave in back then, he now capitulates against his better judgment. He cashes in a small inheritance from his uncle and uses that for the down payment, taking a five-year loan for the balance.

Ryan feels happy—at least for a little while. But each month, when bills come due, he has to juggle funds in order to make the car payment. He's never missed one, but he often asks himself whether it was worth it. The newness of the sports car has worn off, and insurance is expensive. With the extra overtime he has to put in at work, he doesn't even get to drive the car much anymore.

As you can see, the tactic that Ryan used with his mother got the desired results. Thus, he used it often. It was sometimes a battle, but most of the time, it eventually worked. Now Ryan has the same battles within himself. Part of him wants immediate gratification, and another part reminds him of the practicalities. His inner brat doesn't always win as it did with the sports car, but it never gives up trying.

Like Ryan, you probably adopted some preferred strategies for getting your way when you were a child. Those that worked most consistently are the ones that you've kept. Your inner brat isn't exactly the same as Ryan's, but it has similar goals: to maximize pleasure, to get immediate gratification, and to minimize discomfort. All inner brats strive for this; they just use different tactics to get there.

Internal Battles

In the last chapter, you learned that the persona of an inner brat in the midst of interpersonal conflict is usually influenced by your personality style. When it comes to internal battles, the inner brat's tactics are more consistent from one person to the next. These internal battles deal with bad habits such as eating, drinking, or smoking too much; spending money frivolously; getting involved in illicit relationships; and engaging in shoplifting or other illegal, non-assaultive acts. In most people, the internal scenario is usually a variation of "I want it ... but I shouldn't ... but I want it." The intensity and specific content of the words vary from one individual to another, but the main brat persona is almost always the Nag. Most people also experience the Rationalizer in combination with the Nag—although those who act on immediate impulse, without thinking, don't take the time to rationalize. The internal battle is usually the cause (or the result) of bodily tension, followed by a reduction of tension when you succumb.

Think about a habit that you would like to break. Recall that the last time you were faced with a decision about this habit, the urge grew in strength. As it grew, tension in your body began to build. Sensing that you might be giving in to your craving, your Rationalizer inner brat presented a quasi-logical argument that gave you permission to indulge. For example, suppose you were trying to resist buying hot buttered popcorn at the movies, but the aroma was really enticing, at which point the Nag inner brat kept saying, "I've just gotta have that popcorn, even if it does contain 500 calories for the tiny size." At this point, if you hadn't given in yet, your Rationalizer inner brat took over and convinced you that you could exercise tomorrow or skip breakfast. Then it seemed OK to get the popcorn. The tension in your body suddenly dropped; you felt relief. Perhaps you felt a bit of residual guilt, but at that point, you chose to ignore it.

This pattern occurs with regular frequency. The popcorn example is rather trivial compared to other types of cravings. If your only problem was eating too much buttered popcorn, you probably wouldn't be reading this book. Chances are you have considerable trouble resisting more serious urges, such as alcohol, cigarettes, or food in general. Or perhaps you spend more money than you intend to or you gamble too much.

By now it should be apparent that whether it's popcorn or maxing out your credit cards, the mechanism is similar: Your Nag inner brat tries to convince you that you must have whatever it is you're focused on; if that fails, your Rationalizer inner brat provides some reasonable-sounding excuse. It's easy to rationalize one indulgence, such as giving in to your popcorn craving "just this once." However, the popcorn is not the issue. If your goal is to control your behavior, it doesn't matter whether it's popcorn, alcohol, or hard drugs. Once you give in, you've broken a promise to yourself. You've allowed your inner brat to take control.

If you think back to the last time you gave in to your inner brat, you may have felt some relief but not much pleasure or joy. In hindsight, giving in to your impulse probably wasn't worth it, but at the time, it seemed urgent. And it will seem urgent again next time, unless you make some simple changes. These changes include being aware that your inner brat is manipulating you as well as changing what your inner brat is saying.

By now, you should be more aware of the urges that seem like uncontrollable forces within you. You can not only sense them mentally but feel them in your body in the form of tension or other mild discomfort. This discomfort is generated by your inner brat. Once you are aware of this, you can learn to pay attention to more specific details about how your particular inner brat operates.

Your Inner Brat "Talks" to You

The inner brat uses specific tactics to achieve its ends. Whether or not you are aware of it, your inner brat "talks" to you. It is the part of you that says, "I want it" or "I can't stand it" or "I'm entitled."

There is a vast body of research and knowledge on what motivates human beings to do and say things. Some motivators are purely biological reflexes. If you touch a hot stove, your hand withdraws immediately without your needing to think about it. There are few purely biological reflexes that motivate us. For example, hunger and thirst reflect biological needs. When you are famished or parched, your primary focus is to satisfy this need immediately. But will you eat or drink just anything? Perhaps the man wandering in the desert will drink from a muddy pool, but most people in civilized surroundings will not. Therefore, even a strong biological urge is mediated by your thoughts and decisions. Even pain is not reacted to automatically all the time. If you are in the dentist's chair undergoing a delicate and painful procedure, you will not likely move even if the pain seems unbearable.

People have all sorts of cravings. Sometimes they give in to them, while at other times they resist. Suppose you are scheduled for a blood test at 8 A.M., a test which requires that you fast for the previous twelve hours. The night before, you might want a snack, but you ignore the craving, knowing that if you eat anything, the test results will be invalid.

Why is it that sometimes we can feel a strong craving but resist it, while at other times we give in to only mild cravings? The answer lies in what we tell ourselves about the craving. Let's continue the example of craving a snack at night. If we tell ourselves how wonderful the snack will taste or how we just can't get to sleep on an empty stomach, then the craving will intensify. In inner-brat terms, it is your Nag inner brat that is waving these alluring images before your eyes. But if you don't continue a discussion within your mind, if you decide that eating is nonnegotiable, you'll have an easier time resisting the snack. Many people describe such a nonnegotiable attitude as "I just made up my mind."

Whether we give in to cravings depends a lot on how we talk to ourselves. The side of us that really wants or believes it needs to be satisfied is our inner brat. We talk to ourselves more than we realize. We sometimes talk to ourselves out loud, especially when we're trying to concentrate on something. For example, when I'm learning a new skill, such as a dance step, it helps me focus if I narrate what I'm supposed to be doing as I'm doing it: "Right foot, left foot, turn."

Most of the time when we talk to ourselves, however, it is silently in our thoughts. For example, when shopping, you might say to yourself,

"What an original design" or "That's an ugly color." When walking from one room to another, you might be thinking of what you're going to do next. While engaged in a conversation, you might be preparing your comments while the other person is talking.

In general, people don't stop to think about what they're thinking. That is, they are vaguely aware of a running conversation in their minds, but they don't pay attention to it. If you're carrying laundry to the washing machine, you don't usually say to yourself, "I'm carrying laundry to the washing machine." But if someone were to ask you what you were doing, that's what you'd be able to tell them.

There are several "layers" of awareness. If you get shampoo in your eye, you're immediately aware and conscious of what you feel. But other sensations are just below the level of awareness. You probably don't notice the pressure of the watchband on your wrist. Now, if you pay attention to that part of your wrist, you become aware of the faint pressure. If you want to make that pressure even more obvious, try tightening the watchband or moving it up your arm a couple of inches. Notice how aware you are of the sensations on your skin now.

It is the same with your thoughts. You're aware of some of your thoughts, but there are many that you don't notice until you stop and pay attention to what's running through your mind. There are also many thoughts that are not even accessible through reflection. These are your unconscious thoughts. As I pointed out earlier in this book, the unconscious does influence thoughts and feelings, and most people will never uncover what these motives are. Nevertheless, it is not necessary to have complete knowledge of all your deepest mental processes. Research has shown that it is quite possible to get control of your life by zeroing in on thoughts that are at and just below the level of awareness.

Your inner brat operates at these levels. If you pay attention to it, you'll notice that it says all sorts of destructive and manipulative things. Think of the last time you were in a bad mood or when someone said something that upset you. In the back of your mind you were probably engaging in negative self-talk.

Cognitive Therapy

The analysis of such negative self-talk forms the basis for "cognitive" psychotherapy. By figuring out your negative thoughts and assumptions, you can dispute them or address them in other ways in order to change them. For example, if you're upset by someone's comments, you may be saying to yourself, "He shouldn't talk to me that way" or "I must be treated properly, and that other person must be punished." Such thoughts don't really solve anything; they only make you more upset.

The basic premise of cognitive therapy is this: *It is not the situation that upsets you but your reactions to the situation.* This observation was made by the Greek philosopher Epictetus in the first century A.D. Other philosophers, religious leaders, and literary authors have also made reference to the fact that our perceptions color our reactions.

But it was not until the 1950s that this philosophy was brought into the field of psychotherapy, by psychologist Dr. Albert Ellis. While most other therapists were using the psychoanalytic approach—having people talk about anything that came into their mind—Dr. Ellis helped troubled individuals identify the faulty logic in their thinking. While psychoanalysts interacted very little with their patients, allowing them to do most of the talking, Dr. Ellis engaged in active dialogue. He called his method "Rational Emotive Therapy" and later "Rational Emotive Behavior Therapy" (REBT).

Other experts have introduced similar approaches. One of the most notable is Dr. Aaron T. Beck, a psychiatrist who founded the school of Cognitive Behavior Therapy. This approach is similar to REBT in that it also addresses self-defeating thoughts. Although there are some subtle differences in emphasis between the two methods, there is considerable overlap. For the purposes of this book, I will refer to both as the "cognitive" approach, since the emphasis is on what a person assumes and thinks about.

Cognitive therapy has successfully helped millions of people overcome bad habits, depression, anxiety, and even some more serious emotional disorders. Experimental studies have proven that it's not always necessary to undergo intensive, long-term therapy to conquer your problems. It is essential, however, that you be motivated to make the necessary changes in your feelings and your behavior.

As you will see later, you might not be able to change your feelings and your reactions right away, but you *can* change how you behave and what you tell yourself about the situation. With practice, your feelings will eventually correspond more closely with your behavior. For example, let's say you have been assigned the task of selling raffle tickets to raise money for a new organ for your church. Let's further assume that you don't have any particular opinion one way or another about the current organ. It doesn't have the most mellow sound you've ever heard, but it's been adequate. As you approach more and more people to buy a raffle ticket, you find that you become more committed to the cause. That old organ begins to sound shrill to you. You find yourself enthusiastically looking forward to having it replaced with a better one.

Thus, the more you behave in a certain way, the more your beliefs come to conform with your behavior. This process is called "reducing cognitive dissonance." Cognitive dissonance refers to the gap between your current beliefs (i.e., that the organ is perfectly adequate) and what you see yourself doing (selling tickets to raise money for a new organ). These are inconsistent, or dissonant, thoughts. They almost contradict one another. So you have to change one of them. You've already committed yourself to selling the raffle tickets; you're not going to change that. Therefore, you change your thinking in order to bring it more in line with your behavior. It just seems more logical to believe that since you're spending your time soliciting money, it must be for a good cause.

People make these adjustments all the time. Advertisers count on it. When you spend big bucks on an expensive car, for example, you are motivated to convince yourself that it is worth it. Sometimes the Rationalizer inner brat is involved in these internal dialogues.

Summarizing thus far, people talk to themselves within their own minds all the time. They're not always aware of what they're saying to themselves. Sometimes their thoughts are destructive or self-defeating. The cognitive-therapy approach identifies these self-defeating thoughts and helps people find new ways of interpreting situations and making behavioral and emotional changes.

Think of your self-defeating thoughts as the voice of your inner brat. A little brat in the back of your mind is easy to imagine. Everyone knows what a brat is. Just picture whiny, demanding, and selfish behavior. Visualizing such an inner brat brings into focus what you are saying to yourself and what you need to change.

Irrational Assumptions and Cognitive Distortions

Underlying much of your dissatisfaction with yourself and other people are assumptions about the way things should or shouldn't be. Many of these assumptions reflect basic beliefs and "rules" that people impose on themselves and other people. Drs. Beck, Ellis, and others have delineated dozens of such distortions. Here are a few of them. Note their "bratty" tone:

- I must have love and approval from everyone around me. It's awful and terrible if I don't.

- My unhappiness is caused by forces outside of my control, so there is little I can do to feel any better.

- Things must be the way I want them to be. Otherwise, life is intolerable.

- People should always behave the way I want them to. If not, they deserve to be punished.

- Nothing unpleasant, difficult, or frightening should ever happen to me.

- I should never have to feel pain, anger, or other negative emotions. I can't stand these feelings and must eradicate them immediately.

Besides demanding such rules, your mind—specifically the inner brat in your mind—engages in thought processes called cognitive distortions.

These cognitive distortions blow things out of proportion, increasing your internal tension, such that you eventually lose control over your impulses. In his 1980 book *Feeling Good*, David Burns, M.D., describes several types of cognitive distortions.[14] Here are some examples:

- **All-or-nothing thinking.** You see life in extremes. For example, things are either good or bad, wonderful or awful, perfect or worthless. Such thinking renders you intolerant and, therefore, prone to chronic frustration.

- **Overgeneralization.** Because something happened once, you arbitrarily infer it's always going to happen. For example, if a person ignores you for whatever reason, you take that as a sign that the person doesn't care about you at all. Such inferences are not only logically incorrect, but they also make you feel depressed or angry.

- **Mental filter.** You notice only negative details and characteristics in situations. This is the main activity of a pouty or whiny inner brat.

- **Disqualifying the positive.** This is a more extreme variant of the mental filter. You don't ignore positive things, but if you happen to notice them, you turn them into negatives. For example, if you are angry at someone who then does something nice, you tell yourself, "She's just trying to get on my good side."

- **Mind reading.** You make assumptions about what someone else is thinking. For instance, if someone forgets to return your phone call, you assume that he or she must dislike you. When your inner brat thinks this way, it keeps you emotionally isolated from other people.

- *Fortune telling.* You predict all the bad things that will happen in the future. Let's say that on your way to a holiday party, you anticipate that you won't be able to control your drinking. This anticipation gives the inner brat license to indulge its impulses.

- *Emotional reasoning.* If you "feel" something is true, then it surely must be true. For example, if you're afraid of flying, that means planes are unsafe. If you "feel" that your boss is out to hurt you, that means he is. In chapter 6, we saw how Brenda, the self-centered college student, "felt" that the psychologist didn't care about her, a belief that also served as confirmation that he didn't. When the inner brat reasons this way, it disregards observable facts that could offset negative feelings.

- *Magnification.* You exaggerate the negative impact of minor annoyances. Albert Ellis refers to this process as "awfulizing." Minor frustrations are viewed as awful and terrible. The inner brat is an expert at such awfulizing. Awful and terrible things require drastic measures, which are enacted by the inner brat.

The demanding nature of the inner brat almost always involves some type of cognitive distortion as well as a belief or assumption that involves the words "must," "should," "must not," or "should not." For example, "I must be free of discomfort" or "He should not talk to me that way." A couple of corollaries to such assumptions are "It is just awful or terrible when life doesn't turn out the way I want it to" and "I can't stand it."

People who are convinced that they "can't stand" a lot of things are typically very rigid in their thinking. They have an unyielding view of how the world ought to be. Young children are inflexible like this. When my children were very young, I used to make them a snack of celery filled with cream cheese. To make the snack look almost as appetizing as the junk food that they might prefer, I sprinkled a little paprika on the cream cheese. One day I neglected to use the paprika. My children complained that the celery wasn't as it was "supposed to be." In their limited experience, they believed that there was a right and a wrong way to prepare cream-cheese-filled celery, and naked without paprika was definitely the wrong way.

How did you learn to make a peanut-butter-and-jelly sandwich? Did you spread peanut butter on one piece of bread and jelly on the other and then put them together, or did you spread the peanut butter and jelly on the same piece of bread and place the other piece of bread on top? Did you cut the bread into two pieces or four? Rectangles or triangles? Think back to what was *your* version of the "right" way to make a peanut-butter-and-jelly sandwich or any other kind of sandwich.

We all have assumptions, dating back to our childhoods, of how things are supposed to be. Most of us have grown to accept different ways of preparing sandwiches and to be flexible about the outcome. However, there are many other things equally trivial on which we won't budge.

Karen and Her Chicken Soup

Karen had a talent for making chicken soup. She was the neighborhood expert and authority on this form of "Jewish penicillin." Everyone raved about her soup. What special ingredients did she use that made it taste so good? People begged for the recipe. Finally she relented and published the recipe in her synagogue's cookbook. She listed the ingredients in the order that they were to be added to the pot. "But the most important thing," she wrote, "is to cut the wings off the chicken and put them in the pot separately. Under no circumstances should you cook the chicken with the wings on, or it won't taste as good."

Karen's husband couldn't understand why cutting off the wings would make such a difference. "It must have an effect on the way the taste is distributed," Karen assured him. "All I know is that my mother made it that way and so did her mother. It's a secret family recipe." Until people started asking Karen why she cut the wings off the chicken, she had never questioned it. She just assumed that this was the way to make authentic Jewish chicken soup.

But now her curiosity was piqued. She called her mother and asked her, "Mom, you know how you taught me to cook chicken soup? Why do you cut off the wings first?" Her mother replied, "I don't know. That's the way I've always done it. That's how your grandmother did it, and it always tasted delicious. If you really want to know, maybe you should ask her. But don't count on getting an answer. Ever since she entered the nursing home, she hasn't felt much like talking."

A few days later Karen drove over to the nursing home where her grandmother now lived. Grandma was tired but not demented. She was glad to see Karen. After exchanging words of endearment, Karen said, "Grandma, I have something very important to ask you. I need to know the secret." "What secret?" asked her grandmother. "You know, the secret to your chicken soup." "There's no secret," replied her grandmother. "You just throw the chicken in the pot with some water and vegetables and let it simmer for a couple of hours. Don't you know how to make chicken soup?" "Of course I do," answered Karen, "but what's the deal with the wings? I mean, why do you have to cut them off before cooking the chicken?" Her grandmother thought for several long seconds. "Hmm . . ." she said, "hmm . . . I can't recall. Oh, wait a minute—now I remember. My pot was too small to fit the whole chicken, so I had to cut the wings off."

This story illustrates an important point. We get into habits and ways of doing things that we never question. These habits are the "right way," even though we don't know why. Some habits are traditions that for the most part don't cause any disturbance. It doesn't make much difference whether you put on your left shoe first or your right. It is of no consequence whether you dust first or vacuum first or whether you wash the dishes before you wipe off the counters or vice versa. The way that you go about your routine depends partly on how you learned the skills originally. People don't usually change such habits unless they are forced to. It's not only easier but also more efficient mentally not to have to make a decision each time you perform a routine task—up to a point, that is.

Periodically, it doesn't hurt to question whether your typical way of doing something is the most efficient way. I have been reminded of this a few times in my own life. One example occurred several years ago when we got a second dog. I then started buying dry dog food in larger, twenty-five-pound bags. One day, as I was lugging a new—and heavy—bag over to the dogs' bowls, my husband asked me what I was doing. "Their bowls are empty," I replied huffing and puffing so that he might notice how much effort it was and offer to help me. "I have to pour more food in." He chuckled. "Wouldn't it be easier to carry the bowls to the food rather than schlepping that heavy bag around?" Until that moment, such an option had never occurred to me. I had been so locked into the habit of bringing small bags of food over to the bowl and pouring that I continued in this pattern even though it was no longer practical.

They say old habits never die. That holds true not only for how we approach household chores but also in the way we think about things. In my clinical practice, I've worked with countless people who adopted certain ways of thinking when they were young, and they continued to operate from those assumptions even when there was no longer any need to. Marla was one such person. As a child, she was punished whenever she challenged her parents, even about reasonable things, such as "Why do I have to go to bed when it's still light out?" Now in her early thirties, she is still afraid to approach authority. I asked her what her boss could do to her if she asked to take an early lunch break on the day her daughter was singing in a school assembly. She replied that she'd never thought about that before. Once she did think about it, she realized that he couldn't send her to bed without supper, nor would he fire her. The worst he could do would be to say "No." Marla could now see that she had been walking around with this overly cautious attitude for many years longer than necessary. It was time to review and revise some of her assumptions.

Most people carry around old assumptions and expectations, just as Marla did. Some of these assumptions and expectations were at one time logical and useful. For example, if your parents attended to your cries of discomfort within a few minutes, you learned to expect that to continue. And for a while they did. But as I mentioned earlier in this book, all infants and young children have to learn the skill of patience. As you got older, you found that your desires weren't always fulfilled immediately.

The learning process is frustrating. During this time, you probably had your first experience of the feeling of "I can't stand it." That feeling remains today but in new contexts. Thus, even though most of yourself is grown up, your inner brat is still stuck in some of those early, primitive reactions.

Most of your irrational assumptions originate from early childhood, some of them innate, but most of them learned. Your impatience and demanding nature also stem from your early experiences. Whenever you overreact to minor frustrations, it is a repeat performance of your inner brat from hundreds of other frustrating circumstances that came before. The self-absorbed whining, complaining, and anger that you experience today is fueled by old assumptions, expectations, and beliefs that you formed years ago.

According to REBT founder Albert Ellis, if you continue to follow such beliefs, you will make yourself miserable. In fact, he has stated that many people who say they're depressed are actually depressing themselves with their irrational demands and their awfulizing.

Let's review some of the case histories from earlier in this book and examine the process by which people's inner brats engaged in irrational assumptions and cognitive distortions. Remember Dave in chapter 1? He was trying to quit smoking. While going through withdrawal, his inner brat was probably awfulizing his discomfort by complaining that he couldn't stand feeling that way. It may also have been doing some all-or-nothing thinking. In other words, since he didn't feel wonderful, then he must feel terrible.

Think back to Steve, the father who lost his temper over a corn dog. After his tantrum—which no doubt involved some form of "How dare she! I can't stand it!" self-statements—he continued to be grouchy for the rest of the afternoon. His inner brat was operating through a mental filter that focused on only negative aspects of the situation.

Leonard, the sales manager at the car dealership, also engaged in cognitive distortions. After losing his temper with his boss, he went home, complained to his wife about trivial details, sat down with a bottle of booze, and drank himself into a stupor. His overreactions to minor frustrations at home reflected his inner brat's magnification of unimportant events. Later, his self-imposed pity party probably was the result of overgeneralization: because this happened today, it is always going to be this way. Otherwise, why would he have acted as if the situation were hopeless? Leonard's inner brat may also have engaged in some form of mind reading. It may have convinced him that because his boss was displeased with last quarter's sales, the boss probably didn't like him either. All these distortions made Leonard feel more and more miserable.

Cognitive distortions and irrational assumptions give your inner brat more fuel than it deserves. As soon as you start thinking in negative, pessimistic terms, you legitimize your inner brat's self-righteous attitude. It uses those negative thoughts to convince you that there is no other option but to be miserable. It demands that you make the misery stop immediately. And how do you do this? Through some impulsive action, like lashing out at someone or doing something that you'll later regret.

Inner-Brat Attitudes

Besides distorting your perceptions and cognitions, most inner brats adopt a certain attitude of indignation, self-righteousness, or entitlement. Such an attitude is partly a result of the words that your inner brat is saying in the back of your mind. Ideas such as "She has no right to speak to me like that" or "I shouldn't have to wait so long in line" justify the inner brat's intolerance and impatience.

When your inner brat demands something that you know is counter-productive to your own emotional well-being, it boosts its argument by complaining intensely in order to substantiate its position. Suppose, for instance, that you have every intention of going to the gym after work. However, as the day wears on, your enthusiasm for exercise wanes. By the end of the day, you notice that your back hurts or that you feel weak and tired. On the way home, you are still waffling. "Maybe I should wait until tomorrow," you tell yourself. "No, I've really got to be more consistent with exercise." Then your inner brat gets into gear. It reminds you that you've worked hard all day. You're entitled to a rest. Besides, if your back hurts, you don't want to risk injuring it even more. By this time, you're a block from the gym. "Forget it," you say to yourself as you drive by. "Not tonight. I'm much too tired. Besides, I have to write that thank-you note to Aunt Mabel. Life shouldn't have to be so much work."

Here's another example. Let's say you are tempted by the beginnings of an illicit office romance. You are well aware of the trouble that it could lead to. Nevertheless, your inner brat starts obsessing about the person. The desire becomes so great that you are convinced that you "can't help yourself," and you get yourself involved regardless of the potentially destructive consequences. Your inner brat rationalizes the situation by convincing you that other such relationships are trashy, but yours is special, and you shouldn't be deprived of happiness.

Logic isn't very helpful when you're trying to resist an impulse. Almost always the impulse wins out. The inner brat can be very compelling. Recall that earlier I described the inner brat as Cookie Monster with an attitude. If you've watched *Sesame Street,* you know that Cookie Monster walks around growling for cookies. You can probably think of at least a half-dozen situations in the recent past where you operated on pure emotion or impulse. Perhaps it was a fit of anger, or an "attack of the munchies," as we say about specific snack cravings. Or maybe it was procrastination in getting started on a major project. Sometimes all the reasoning in the world doesn't seem to make you want to do what you know is best for yourself

Many people just resign themselves to their impulses. They figure they have no other choice. They may blame it on bad genes, on a "chemical imbalance" in the brain, or on other factors beyond their control. It is true that genes and chemicals play a role in determining some of our characteristics and propensities. But this doesn't mean that we can't make adjustments.

The more you give in to your inner brat, the less likely you are to accomplish what you set out to do and the more frustrating will be your relationships with other people. Furthermore, although you may get what you want in the short term, you will never feel a sense of satisfaction with life in general. Long-term goals will never be accomplished when the inner brat is in control.

Furthermore, if we all gave in to our inner brats, our society would be in a sorry state. A community can thrive only when there is cooperation. And cooperation sometimes requires curbing your own impulses for the benefit of the group. When you learn techniques for self-regulation, not only will you be happier and more productive and have greater self-esteem, but you will also contribute to greater harmony with others and have more satisfying relationships.

10

How to Identify Your Inner Brat: Signs That Your Inner Brat Is in Control

Taming your inner brat is most effective when you recognize its manipulations early in a situation. Once you're deep into inner-brat territory, it is more difficult to stop. In this chapter, you will find specific guidelines for identifying inner-brat thoughts, feelings, and behaviors so that you can make necessary adjustments. But first, let's discuss what your inner brat is *not*.

What the Inner Brat Is *Not*

The inner brat is not a psychiatric diagnosis. It's merely a convenient way of describing the psychological mechanism by which people fail to control their urges and impulses. Everyone has an inner brat. It is not a mental disorder.

The inner brat is not a substance or chemical in the brain. It cannot be seen under x-ray or by other imaging techniques, nor can it be measured directly. The quiz in chapter 7 was not a precise calibration of any physical matter. It was designed only as a guide to help you identify some of your counterproductive patterns of thinking and behaving.

The inner brat is not to be confused with serious emotional disturbances such as severe depression, suicidal thoughts, bipolar disorder, obsessive-compulsive disorder, schizophrenia, and other psychiatric conditions. The inner brat may contribute to these conditions, but it is not the main cause. If you have serious problems with your emotions, such as chronic, crippling fears; pervasive suspiciousness; or profound and unrelenting sadness, you need more help than this book can provide. If you can't get yourself up in the morning, if you've lost all interest in things, if you have trouble sleeping, if you feel confused a lot, you may need and should seek professional help.

The foregoing is not a complete list of symptoms that require professional help. It is not meant to substitute for a live evaluation. However, if you are in doubt, I encourage you to consult a mental-health professional. Get a referral from your clergyman, from a physician, or from a friend or relative who can recommend someone. If you prefer, call the American Psychological Association's "Talk to Someone Who Can Help" line (1-800-964-2000, United States and Canada only), and they will refer you to a psychologist in your area. If you do not live in the United States or Canada, contact your national psychological association or local mental-health facility.

What's the Difference between the Inner Brat and Just Plain Old Spontaneity?

Impulsiveness is what drives the inner brat, but not all impulsiveness constitutes inner-brat behavior. Spontaneity is the positive side of impulsiveness. For example, when you're on your way to a movie and decide on the spur of the moment to go to a museum instead, that is an impulsive, spontaneous decision, but it is not a bratty one. On the other hand, if you're on your way to your girlfriend's house to apologize for something and then suddenly change your mind and go to a museum instead, that is brattiness. The difference is that, in the first example, there is no specific intent on doing something that you have decided is the "right" thing to do. How you spend your leisure is a matter of preference; there is no right or wrong. In the second example, however, you have decided to do the right thing (that is, apologize to your girlfriend), but at the last minute you back out. You may feel relief at the moment, but later you'll be disappointed with yourself. This disappointment is a sign that your inner brat was involved in your decision.

What's the Difference between Self-Concern and Self-Absorption?

Differentiating between normal self-concern and narcissistic self-absorption is often difficult. If you read a self-help book, are you too self-absorbed? If you decide to have cosmetic dental work, are you being narcissistic? What about Olympic hopefuls who train several hours per day and who must pay close attention to minor fluctuations in their bodies' muscle tone, balance, and nutrition?

Wanting to improve yourself or pursue a personal goal is not narcissistic per se. It becomes so, however, when you feel entitled to special attention or treatment because of it. If you expect other people to adapt to your agenda, you are too self-absorbed. For example, suppose you decide to start going to the gym after work every day and won't be home until 8 P.M. If you insist that your family wait for you for dinner, when they have been used to eating at 6 P.M., you are being self-centered. To demand that everyone accommodate you for your convenience is characteristic of your inner brat.

There is nothing wrong with self-improvement. However, when you become obsessed with it, you lose touch with what's important. I know people who have had one cosmetic surgery after another: breast reduction or enlargement, liposuction, collagen lip implants, Botox injections to get rid of lines. They do not need these surgeries. They are not in movies or on television and subject to the critical scrutiny of an industry that demands physical perfection. They are regular folks who are unhappy with their looks. Those who have multiple cosmetic surgeries are so self-absorbed that they exaggerate their physical flaws. It is not surprising that they are disappointed when the surgeries do not rid them of their emotional dissatisfaction.

Self-absorption is not the same as self-reflection. Reflecting about your place in the world and reviewing your relationships with other people are normal and useful activities. But to dwell on what others have done to you or to brood about your disappointments is counterproductive. That is when the thoughts of your narcissistic inner brat work against you.

Signs That Your Inner Brat Is in Control

There are several signs or signals that your inner brat is in control. Here are some of the most common:

You find yourself getting angry over something that later seems trivial. One of the most common circumstances in which such irrational anger occurs is while you are in traffic or while you are waiting in line. In these situations, time passes very slowly. Waiting one minute for the traffic light to turn green seems like an eternity. Watching an elderly lady in front of you in line trying to find a quarter at the bottom of her purse can be agonizing in its slowness. Most people in a hurry will feel at least a bit frustrated or impatient but will not necessarily make themselves upset by it.

If you find yourself getting angry or if you feel your bodily tension rising to the point where you feel you might explode if you don't do something about it, then your inner brat is at work. If you're not sure whether you are overreacting or being unreasonable, ask yourself whether most other people would react in the same way. Or look around you to see how others are behaving.

You are cynical or sarcastic. People who are cynical usually dwell on the negative. They don't expect things to turn out well. Those who use sarcasm say things that sound innocent but are meant to hurt others. If this style describes you, then your inner brat is in a constant pout. People may try to cheer you up, but you won't let them. For some reason, your inner brat wants to stay mad.

You wallow in resentment or jealousy. It's perfectly normal to feel resentful, envious, or jealous. Although we are taught to not compare ourselves with others, it is human nature to do so. Civilized societies depend on group norms to keep people's behaviors within acceptable limits. Young children learn skills and other behaviors (both positive and negative) from watching older children and comparing their own behavior with that of their peers. When you hear that a professional football player can earn

$100,000 or more *per game*, it's almost impossible not to compare that with your own modest salary and to feel at least a twinge of envy.

However, if you spend more than a few moments on this envy, you are giving your inner brat too much latitude. If you dwell on resentments and feel sorry for yourself because the other guy has it easier, then you are allowing your inner brat to control you.

You feel hurt and dwell on it. It is not unusual to feel hurt by someone's words or actions. We've all been there. But the inner brat can take that emotional pain and, through cognitive distortion, magnify it out of proportion. Suppose a co-worker took sole credit for a project that you had worked on together. That is certainly disappointing, and you may even feel betrayed. Most people would. However, if you complain about this disappointment to your spouse, your three best friends, and your online chat room, your inner brat is getting way too much mileage out of it. You will only end up feeling worse.

You hold grudges. If after having been slighted, ignored, or hurt by someone, you stay angry for a long time, it is because your inner brat keeps reviewing the situation that upset you, playing it like a tape, over and over. The longer it plays, the more justified you feel in staying angry. People who hold grudges sometimes say, "I can forgive, but I can't forget." When I ask them what they mean, their explanation reveals that they haven't forgiven at all. To forgive is to truly put the grudge to rest. When you keep recalling it, the grudge is still active, kept alive by your inner brat.

You frequently plot revenge against someone who may not even be aware that you have been hurt. This kind of brooding is similar to the grudge-holding in the preceding description, except that you plan to take action on your grudge. When you nurse your anger and plan ways to get back at someone, there is a closed information loop in your mind. That is, your feelings and your reactions are based on the assumptions you previously made about the situation. In such a closed loop, you have no means of verifying those assumptions. Here's an example: One of my clients told me about her experience when a co-worker's car was in the shop for several days for major repairs. She offered to pick him up on the way to work, and he accepted. He did not offer to help pay for gas. At the end of the week, he announced, "My car will be ready today. I won't need a ride anymore." My client felt hurt that he didn't at least thank her for her help, let alone offer to pay for gas. But she didn't say anything. She decided to let it go. But her inner brat wouldn't let it go. It dwelled on her co-worker's ingratitude and inconsiderateness. All day she couldn't get her mind off the many ways in which she would make him "pay" for this transgression. Imagine her chagrin when she arrived home that night and found a beautiful bouquet of flowers and a thank-you note sent by the man she had driven to work for the past week.

You end up regretting what you said or did. This happens most frequently with behaviors and habits that you have been trying to control. If, for example, you have been trying to subdue your temper, you will feel badly after an outburst. If you are trying to lose weight or to quit smoking or drinking but succumb to your urges, it is your inner brat that has brought you to that point.

Keep in mind that not all people who eat, drink, or smoke too much do so because of an inner brat. If they feel no guilt in doing so, their inner brat is not active at the times they indulge. Even people who are trying to curb their habits sometimes give themselves advance "permission" to splurge, such as when they go on vacation. When they are not trying to restrict themselves, the inner brat is not a factor.

You end up regretting what you didn't say or do. How many times have you told yourself, "I must sew that button on my shirt" or "I really need to confront the guy who keeps parking in my spot"? Every day, people think of dozens of things that need to get done, but they don't get around to accomplishing them. This is simple procrastination. You promise yourself you'll do something, but you usually end up finding an excuse not to do it. The inner brat is at work here, probably whining in the back of your mind that it's too much effort or trying to rationalize putting off the task until later.

You walk around feeling angry and dissatisfied. People who are chronically dissatisfied usually feel like victims. They blame other people and situations for their problems. Their inner brats refuse to acknowledge that they, themselves, have contributed to their own unhappiness. Think of a "fussy" baby. If that's how you feel much of the time, your inner brat needs to be tamed. As mentioned earlier, if you are so unhappy that you can't seem to get through the day, then this state of mind is more than your inner brat. In this case you probably need professional help.

You feel guilty. Sometimes, but not always, guilt reflects your awareness that you've hurt someone. The inner brat is not involved in the guilt part but in the transgression that preceded the guilt. Let's say you betrayed a friend's confidence. Even before she finds out, you may feel guilty. Not only do you regret what you did, but it eats away at you for a long time.

Keep in mind that some people feel unrealistically guilty. That is, they feel responsible for something they didn't cause. In such situations, it's debatable whether the inner brat is involved; the problem may be due to other psychological factors.

You don't want anyone to know about something you're doing. Except for planning a surprise party, a business deal, or another event that requires secrecy, there is no reason to hide certain actions unless you feel guilty about them or you know that they're wrong. If you are eating, drinking, or smoking in secret, you are under the control of your inner brat. If you engage in shoplifting, stalking, or voyeurism, you are paying too much heed to your inner brat.

You find yourself frequently disappointed by the people around you. If it seems that everyone lets you down or that people just can't be trusted, then either you run with a really nasty crowd or there is something about you that makes you continually disappointed. Perhaps it is your inner brat's unrealistic expectations of what other people are supposed to do for you. Or perhaps it is your own inflated sense of importance.

You have no friends. No one seems to like you. Imagine a whiny child complaining that he has no friends. If you were to observe this child on the playground, you would not see him approaching other children. Instead, he'd stand or wander around by himself. Adults who complain about not having friends act similarly. They don't approach anyone and then wonder why nobody seems interested in them.

If you feel this way, it's because of two possibilities: either you are afraid to approach people, or you believe that you shouldn't have to seek out company. The inner brat is responsible in both situations. In the first situation, your fear is magnified by your inner brat. Nothing terrible will happen if you walk up to someone and start talking, even though your inner brat tries to convince you that you will be shamed beyond hope. In the second situation, your inner brat is trying to capitalize on its sense of entitlement. It says to you, "People should come to me. I shouldn't have to beg for their attention."

You complain a lot about the unfairness of situations. Who says life must be fair? It is not written in the Ten Commandments, in the United States Constitution, or in any other document or law. It must be your inner brat which demands that life be fair. Implicit in the phrase "It's not fair" is the expectation that "You owe me," that you are entitled to be compensated.

This expectation has honest roots in childhood. At a certain point in a child's life, around the age of eight or nine years, fairness is an important issue. This is when children organize their own games and try to play within an accepted set of rules. Those who don't play by the rules are quickly ostracized. Fairness is also reinforced within one's family, where typically the parents try to give equal time and resources to each of their children. Thus, if Johnny gets a piece of cake, Susie must have exactly the same size piece, or else "It's not fair."

It would be nice if the world worked that way, but it doesn't. Your inner brat hasn't learned that not everyone has access to all available opportunities and rewards. When it sees someone else getting more than you or when you get caught speeding while the other guys got away, your inner brat wallows in self-pity.

You have to justify your behavior to yourself or to someone else. If one person nags you or accuses you of something, you may or may not be in the wrong. However, when several people find fault with you about the same thing, then there's a good chance you are at fault. If you have to justify your actions to a lot of people, then your inner brat is making you difficult to live with. You may be acting selfishly or inconsiderately.

Suppose, for instance, that at home you're constantly reminded to clean up after yourself, and at work you're admonished for not putting supplies back where they belong. Suppose further that your friends complain you're always late. Now, you could ask yourself, "Why is everyone on my case?" But a better question would be, "How is my inner brat distracting me from being considerate?" Your inner brat may relish its independence from other people's control, but the price you pay is frequent conflict with others.

You feel slighted when the focus of attention is not on you. Some inner brats want so much to be the center of attention that they develop a hostile attitude when they're not. I know someone who solicits compliments and reassurance from other people. When the focus is on her, she is pleasant and animated. However, when praise is directed toward someone else, she becomes quiet and sullen. Her inner brat is probably telling her that it can't stand not being noticed.

If you resent attention paid to other people, if you feel hurt when someone doesn't try to humor you when you're irritable, your inner brat is responsible for this.

You make a lot of critical comments or spread gossip about other people. Most people who are critical of others are dissatisfied with themselves. Finding fault with other people is a way of displacing your own discontent. Think back to the last time you were in a bad mood. No matter how beautiful the weather or how stress-free your day was, you would have found something to complain about. On the other hand, when you're in a good mood, even a blizzard can't easily make you unhappy, and even a hectic day does not have as negative an impact. When you're in the negative state, you're under the influence of your inner brat.

The foregoing is not an exhaustive list of all the signs that your inner brat is in control. It would be impossible to anticipate every individual's personal response to various thoughts and situations. However, you do get a sense of how formidable and pervasive the inner brat can be.

In general, your inner brat reflects your own self-absorption combined with behavioral impulses that you would disrespect if you saw them in other people. It is easy to spot bratty behavior in other people because you are more logical and objective about other people than you are about yourself. When you're not emotionally worked up, you can see the irrational nature of other people's words and actions.

It's much more difficult to notice your own errors in judgment when you are under the influence of your inner brat. When your inner brat is in control, you are too focused on your own wishes and feelings. You don't view the facts objectively. The inner brat rejects logic and rationality. It reacts from primitive emotion, even though another part of you "knows better." If your own inner brat is so difficult to spot, does this mean you'll never get it under control? No. Just because it is difficult to see your own inner brat, identifying it is by no means impossible. At first, you'll realize only after the fact that your inner brat was in control—after you yelled at your children, or after you polished off the ice cream, or after you put off paying bills for yet another day. When you think back to what happened, you then can view it as a product of your inner brat.

Once you become proficient at identifying inner-brat thoughts and behaviors in hindsight, you'll be able to catch yourself in the middle of such thoughts and behaviors. With practice, you may even be able to prevent your inner brat from getting started in some situations.

You may already be aware of inner-brat thoughts and behaviors while they are happening. You may also notice that being aware of your inner brat doesn't necessarily mean being able to stop it. In the next chapter, you'll learn about conditions and circumstances that interfere with your stopping the inner brat. These conditions give the inner brat a powerful edge over your own logic.

11

Circumstances That Give Your Inner Brat the Edge: How to Protect Yourself

You are now aware of the potentially destructive actions of your inner brat. In its pursuit of maximizing pleasure and minimizing discomfort, it can sabotage your best intentions for self-control. With its narcissistic focus and demand for immediate gratification, it can wreak havoc in your relationships with other people. The inner brat is that primitive part of yourself which never matured, a vestige from your infancy and early childhood.

In the last chapter, I presented typical thoughts, feelings, and behaviors that reflect the action of the inner brat. Brooding, holding a grudge, complaining, overreacting, continual dissatisfaction, and other indicators should alert you that your inner brat has a grip on you. Once you recognize this grip, you can mentally intervene to interrupt the inner brat. But as I pointed out, this is not always easy. When you are in the throes of your inner brat, you may realize that you're being unreasonable, but like a bratty child, your inner brat will protest, "I don't care. I'm going to do it anyway."

I have experienced such feelings myself in many situations. When frustrated over some minor inconvenience, I might try to say to myself rationally, "Now, you know that you're being a brat." "So what?" I retort to myself, "I don't care." Or when I procrastinate, I know precisely what is happening to me psychologically, but that does not make me want to jump right in and complete the task that I've been putting off for weeks. Even though I know why I behave a certain way, that awareness is not sufficient to change the behavior.

If all it took was awareness and knowledge to change ourselves, everyone would be close to perfect. There are certainly enough self-help books, personal trainers, executive coaches, therapists, and other advisors who can tell us what's wrong and why.

People intend to make changes but don't follow through. We see this every year on January 1, the date of the big New Year's Resolution. At the gym where I exercise, I see huge crowds every January. People have decided once and for all to get into shape. By mid-February, the crowds have dissipated significantly. There's no waiting for the exercise machines, and the attendant no longer runs out of towels.

More diets begin on January 1 than at any other time of year. People resolve to quit smoking and drinking as well. Most people who make these resolutions do so after careful deliberation, having planned well in advance to change their behavior. Few will be successful. With all this careful planning, you'd expect a much higher success rate. When I ask people why they don't continue an exercise program, they typically say, "I don't have time."

When I ask why they keep losing their temper, they usually reply, "I was provoked; I couldn't help it." When I ask why they haven't quit drinking or smoking, they answer, "I meant to, but something happened that set me off."

Do you notice a pattern in these responses? They all refer to forces outside the person. Very few people would answer those questions honestly by saying, for instance, "It was more important for me to sit and watch television rather than to exercise," "I failed to control myself," or "I just wanted to have a drink." As described in chapter 3, we tend to attribute our shortcomings to temporary, situational factors. This reasoning preserves a sense of self-esteem, but it's not necessarily an accurate view of how things really are.

Most of our problems with following through on goals are due to failure at self-control or self-regulation. Some people call it a lack of willpower, but that's only part of it.

Willpower

What is willpower? Dictionaries define it as self-control, resolve, discipline, and other similar terms. These words all imply a sense of self-denial, or "won't" power, as in, "I won't give in to temptation." While not inaccurate, this definition does leave out an important element. What are people doing when they're not giving in to temptation? What are they doing instead?

Psychologists have studied what determines self-control. Willpower involves changing the priorities of your behavioral tendencies. In almost every situation, there is more than one choice of what to do. Suppose, for instance, that you're at home by yourself and you suddenly feel an irritating itch on your arm. You have a choice. You can scratch it, rub it, hit it, or ignore it. In all likelihood, you will just scratch it without giving it much thought. But let's say this itch occurred while you were carrying a heavy box of fragile items. You wouldn't scratch immediately. First, you'd put the box down or else carry it to its destination. In other words, while carrying the box, you have competing priorities: to not drop the box and to relieve your itch. You can't accomplish both goals at the same time, so you have to choose one over the other.

What you end up doing in most situations depends on which behavioral tendency is the most probable in that context. In this example, the itch gets your attention, which makes scratching a highly probable response—*unless* something else competes with that probability. In this case, it is the desire to not drop the box. Now protecting the fragile items becomes a higher priority than scratching your itch, at least temporarily.

Or suppose that the itch is in your crotch. If your are at home, you probably wouldn't hesitate to scratch it. But if you are in an elevator with a stranger, you would not likely scratch. Instead, you might squirm around or try to think of something else to tide you over until you are alone. Thus, your urge to scratch would have been overridden by a desire to not embarrass yourself.

Willpower is a matter of recognizing different possible responses to a given situation. You then make a conscious choice to not do what would ordinarily be your most likely behavior and, next, to replace that behavior with an alternative response that is still acceptable. The typical goal is to bypass the desire for immediate gratification in order to achieve something that benefits you more in the long run.

Here is an example: Suppose you are tired from a long day, but there is a stack of bills that you've been putting off, and you face penalties and interest if you don't have them in the mail by tomorrow. Usually, when you're tired, you wouldn't choose to pay bills. However, if avoiding penalties and interest is a priority, you will find the energy to write the checks. The more probable behavior of relaxing is overridden by a less probable but more important priority.

Or let's say someone brings big, delicious-looking cookies to work and invites you to have some. If you've made a commitment to losing weight, you have at least two competing responses. One, of course, is to satisfy your sweet tooth. The other is to fit into your old jeans. Depending on which response tendency is stronger at the moment, you will either take a cookie or else say, "No thanks." Willpower comes into play when you mentally adjust the priorities. Even though the cookies smell delicious and you want one—or two, or five—you convince yourself that it's more important to fit into your jeans in a few weeks than it is to have a cookie right now.

Thus, willpower is not simply restraint. It involves mental processes whereby you consider alternative courses of action and choose that which is best for you in the long run, even though another alternative may seem more immediately attractive. When you lose willpower, you don't really "lose" anything. You have merely made the choice to give in to your desire for immediate gratification or relief instead of following your plan for long-term benefit.

Obstacles against Change

Even with our best intentions, we often make bad choices. How many times have you promised yourself that you will stick to your diet today or that you'll start working on your income tax tonight, and then you end up not living up to your commitment? If this happens frequently, you need to examine not only what your inner brat is saying to you internally but also what other conditions in the environment or within your own body make it harder to control your urges.

Some of these factors are described by psychologist Roy Baumeister and his colleagues, who have been researching the area of self-control and how and why we lose it.[15] They propose that self-control operates somewhat like a muscle.

Here's an analogy. When you exert yourself physically, such as by moving furniture all day, you're tired. At the end of such a day, you don't usually feel like going out to play tennis. Similarly, when you try to control behavior in one area of your life, such as resisting the urge to smoke, that also depletes you of energy—not in a physical sense but in your mental ability to cope with other challenges.

Dr. Baumeister and his colleagues demonstrated this phenomenon in several laboratory experiments. For example, people who were sitting by plates of chocolate candies and freshly-baked chocolate-chip cookies, but who had been told not to eat them, did more poorly in a subsequent puzzle task than those who did not have such a restriction. The people who had been tempted by the sweets did not persist as long on the puzzle. It was as if their mental energy was depleted from resisting the cookies and candies.

It is interesting to note that controlling the urge to reach for a cookie had a negative impact on a later activity that had nothing to do with food. That is, when you exercise self-control in one part of your life, you may not have enough strength left to maintain control in other situations.

Generalizing to everyday circumstances, this research suggests that if you are actively vigilant in dieting, quitting smoking, or moderating your drinking, you "use up" some internal strength, leaving you at a disadvantage to cope with other stressors. This depletion of strength explains why people are more irritable when they are trying to quit smoking or lose weight. Their vigilance and self-control over their habit depletes their strength to control their tempers.

The good news is that—just as with muscles—when you rest for a while, your strength returns. Indeed, Dr. Baumeister has proposed that, with practice, you can build up your strength and stamina, just as a weight trainer builds strength with regular exercise. This effect is further explained in the next chapter, but first let's examine some factors that deplete you of strength to cope with your inner brat.

Fatigue

It takes a lot of energy to change yourself. Think back to the last time you tried to lose weight, quit smoking, stop spending money, etc. In order to jump-start yourself, you had to monitor your behavior closely. You had to pay close attention to where you went and what you did or did not do, so as to ensure that you wouldn't lapse into old behavior patterns. That can be exhausting.

It's not unexpected that New Year's resolutions begin so ambitiously and fail so abruptly. People underestimate the energy that it takes to exercise self-discipline. When they feel drained, they give up—in the same way that they would if they were trying to lug a huge boulder across town.

When mentally or physically tired, you lack the energy to exert control over your impulses. This fatigue makes you more vulnerable to your

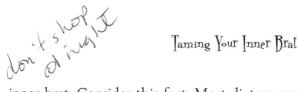

inner brat. Consider this fact: Most dieters overeat at night when they're tired. Most impulsive crimes also take place at night. It seems that restraints on behavior tend to break down as the day wears on.

To understand how fatigue allows the inner brat to flourish, consider how an exhausted parent reacts to a whiny child. At the supermarket on a Friday night, observe parents in the checkout line. (You may even be one of them!) The ones with the fatigue lines on their faces give in to their children's whining for treats because they feel too tired from the long week to deal with the consequence of saying "No."

Assuming that your inner brat acts much like a whiny child, you tend to react to it in the manner described above. That is, when you are tired, you have trouble finding the energy to override your desires for immediate gratification.

Stress

Stress comes in many forms. It can originate from outside yourself or from within. External stressors include hectic schedules; continuous noise or interruption; physical illness or injury; and major losses, such as unemployment, divorce, or death of a loved one. Situations such as these demand extraordinary adjustments and coping skills, so they drain you of energy.

Another form of stress is that which comes from within your own mind, such as worrying. When you worry about something that has not yet occurred and that may never occur, you feel apprehensive; you likely experience tension in some part of your body as well. Worrying is an internal stressor that takes over your whole being.

The difference between an external stressor, such as a fire in your living room, and an internal one is that with the external stressor there is a real, objective, and usually immediate irritant or threat. If you don't do something about the fire, you might die. On the other hand, when you worry about flying in a plane, there is not necessarily any danger. Recall the section on emotional reasoning in chapter 9. This cognitive distortion implies, "Because I am afraid, there must be danger." Worrying is a self-imposed stressor. The threat comes not from a verifiable, objective situation but from your own thoughts.

In terms of its effects on the body, it turns out that there is almost no difference between an external and internal stressor. That is, worrying about being attacked can be almost as stressful as actually watching an attacker coming toward you. In both situations, you feel as if you have no control. In both situations, your body reacts by producing stress hormones and other reactions to prepare you for self-defense. Your mind becomes overly focused on the immediate concern. Such reactions are holdovers from primitive times when people had to be ready to fight attackers or flee from them in an instant.

Thus, even when you are in no immediate physical danger you might still be under stress that comes from cognitive distortions. You know how draining this stress can be. When your attention and energy are siphoned off by stress, you have little stamina left. If you are trying to cope with your inner brat at the same time, you will be only minimally successful at best.

Inertia

In the ordinary sense, *inertia* refers to something that isn't moving. One example that comes to mind is the *inertia* which prevents me from getting up off the couch when I don't feel like doing much of anything. But if you recall your high school physics class, you'll remember that the technical definition of *inertia* is "a tendency to remain in the state one is in." That means if you're sitting, the law of inertia dictates that you will stay sitting. But if you are moving, the law of inertia keeps you moving. Thus, if you're in a car that comes to a sudden stop, you will keep moving forward for a second or so; if you don't have a seatbelt on, you might go through the windshield.

What does this have to do with the inner brat? Just as it is hard to prevent yourself from lunging forward in a car that stops suddenly, it is difficult to stop your inner brat once it engages itself in action. If you've taken one bite of a brownie, it's very hard to resist taking another—unless you use certain mental strategies that I'll describe in the next chapter. Once your mouth starts chewing, your inner brat wants it to keep going, even after you tell yourself to stop. Furthermore, the longer your inner brat pursues its desires, the harder it is to stop. This loss of resolve is due to psychological inertia. It is the principle underlying binge eating and binge drinking. It is especially relevant if you have an all-or-nothing approach to self-control. "What the heck," you might say to yourself, "I've already broken my diet, so there's nothing I can do now."

This snowballing phenomenon was first demonstrated experimentally by psychologists C. P. Herman and D. Mack in 1975.[16] They told their subjects not to eat before the experiment. The researchers first gave them either one, two, or three milkshakes. Later, they gave them two bowls of ice cream to taste-test. The purpose of the experiment was initially kept secret from the subjects. While they thought the objective was to give their opinions on ice-cream flavors, in reality it was to see how much ice cream they ate after being "pre-loaded" with milkshakes.

Who do you think ate the most ice cream? If you've never dieted, you might guess that the subjects who had only one milkshake ate the most ice cream, because they were probably still hungry. This was the case for the subjects who didn't worry about their weight. But for those who were on a diet, the ones who had *three* milkshakes ate more ice cream than those who had only one. Whenever I mention this study to an audience, I usually see several heads nodding, as if to say, "Yeah, I can understand that." You see, it has nothing to do with hunger. When you have a mindset that you are either *on* your diet or *off*, then as soon as you take that first sip of milkshake, you are *off* the diet and cease even trying to control yourself. Psychological inertia keeps you eating once you've started.

We see psychological inertia in action not only with excessive eating but also with drinking, gambling, and shopping, especially when people subscribe to the all-or-nothing approach to self-control. You probably know people who don't stop at one or two drinks, who stay at the bar until closing time. Gamblers face similar inertia. It takes a lot of restraint to gamble only a little bit. Compulsive shoppers also have trouble stopping at one or two items. They may buy only one or two items at a time, but their minds are focused on the next purchase. Psychological inertia also occurs during temper tantrums and tirades. Once some people start yelling, they can't seem to stop.

Attention

In order to control your inner brat, you must first be aware of it. This awareness requires paying attention to it. You must be aware of what it is whining or complaining about, what it is nagging you to do or not to do, and so on. Attending to these mental processes is productive, because self-monitoring is instrumental in achieving self-control.

Too often, however, people pay attention to the wrong things. For example, while it's important to be aware of what your inner brat is saying to you, you don't want to give it a great deal of "air time" because that will only increase the inner brat's power. When you pay too much attention to it, you lose your objective focus.

Think back to a situation where you couldn't get something off your mind. It might be a song that wouldn't stop echoing in your head, an image of a cigarette or of a juicy burger smothered in melted cheese. Or it may have been jealousy or thoughts of revenge toward someone who betrayed you. The reason that such thoughts stay in your mind is that you pay attention to them. In a sense, such fixation is your inner brat at work. It dwells on what it craves and what it blames.

You could try saying to yourself, "Well, if that bothers you, just stop thinking about it. Stop paying attention to it." I don't know about you, but such reasoning has never worked for me or anyone I know. In a series of experiments by psychologist Daniel Wegner and his colleagues, subjects were told not to think of a white bear. Not unexpectedly, they found that the more that people tried *not* to think of a white bear, the more they actually did think about it.[17]

A subsequent experiment by psychologist Mark Muraven and others first instructed subjects to write down their thoughts on a piece of paper and to avoid thinking of a white bear. They then showed the subjects a comedy videotape and told them not to smile, laugh, or show any other emotions. These subjects had a harder time suppressing their subsequent emotional reactions than did the control group, who were initially given arithmetic problems and no mention of any white bears. These results imply that trying to not think about something (in this case, a white bear) uses up mental strength. Immediately afterwards, there is not enough strength to suppress emotions.[18]

In another experiment, Dr. Muraven and his colleagues demonstrated a sobering observation. The participants in the study were instructed to try not to think of white bears and then told that they would be taking a driving-simulation test in which they could win a prize for good performance. Control-group participants were not initially told anything about white bears. Before taking the test, both groups of subjects were given a chance to drink beer. Now, consider that all participants in the study were expecting to take a driving-simulation test. Knowing the link between drinking and driving, you'd expect that they would all control the amount they drank. However, the subjects who had been instructed to suppress their thoughts ended up drinking more than those in the control group. Their mental energy had been depleted, such that they later exercised less control over their drinking, even when they knew that their driving skills were going to be tested.[19] Although this was a laboratory experiment, it does have implications for real life. It is not too far-fetched to predict that when you try to avoid certain thoughts and ideas, you are less adept at controlling your drinking immediately afterwards. It gives new meaning to the phrase, "I drink to forget."

What the preceding studies confirm is something that we already know intuitively. That is, the more you focus on control, the less control you actually have. When you direct your attention to not eating a particular food that is on the table, you seem to want it more. When you try to muster all your self-control to try not to scratch an itch, it seems to itch even more intensely. When you try to forget about your spouse's past lovers, the images appear even more vividly. Furthermore, these attempts to control your attention leave you less strength to deal with other areas of your life.

The more you pay attention to something you're trying to avoid, the less successful you will be at avoiding it. Even when you think you're successfully forcing something out of your mind, you are still vulnerable to a "rebound" effect. In his experiments on suppressing "white bear" thoughts, Dr. Wegner found that after a period of trying not to think of white bears, and then encouraged to do so, people thought about bears even more than they had before. It seems that whether you obsess about something or try very hard not to obsess, you are using up mental strength.

In inner-brat terms, trying not to think of something that's in your mind is akin to opposing your inner brat. It wants to think about it, while you try to suppress it. This conflict sets you up for a power struggle in the same way as when you are arguing with an actual bratty child. Imagine this conversation with a bratty child:

"Stop that."

"No."

"I said stop it right now."

"Make me."

"I mean it. You'd better stop that right now."

"I don't have to."

And so on. You can see how fruitless such a conversation is.

One important aspect of attention has to do with where it is directed. If you pay too much attention to current discomfort, you lose sight of your long-term goals. In other words, if you pay too much attention to a craving, you ignore the reason you're abstaining. If you focus too much on how angry you are, you don't think enough about the consequences of following through on that anger. For this reason, some people get into fights that land them in jail. They have their mind so fixed on getting even with the person who insulted them that they don't consider the possibility of getting arrested. (This rationale may also explain why the death penalty is not an effective deterrent against murder.)

Situational Cues

Another obstacle that stands in the way of your controlling your inner brat is a concept called *mental association*. We associate certain cues in the environment with certain behaviors. I sometimes joke that I'm on a "see-food" diet. When I see food, I eat it. The availability of food serves as a signal to eat. We all respond to various situational cues. It's more efficient that way. You don't have to plan and ponder your actions as much. If you're driving along and you approach a gas station, you might check your gauge to see if you need to fill up. If you pass a video store, you may remind yourself to return the movie that's due. If you arrive home and leave the key in the ignition when you open the car door, your car may emit a sound that signals you to remove the key. These are all helpful situational cues; they don't trigger any potentially destructive behaviors.

But some situational cues do encourage bad habits. For example, smokers usually associate the end of a meal with lighting up a cigarette, because this routine has been a habit. Thus, to a smoker, the meal is not complete until he's had his cigarette. Other people associate walking in their front door with going to the kitchen for a snack, even if they're not hungry. A person who is trying to quit drinking would best stay away from bars and taverns. If you've spent a lot of time in such places, then just being in a bar increases your urge to drink, because that's the behavior you associate with being in a bar.

Mental associations don't only trigger behaviors. They also evoke feelings. Have you noticed the television commercials for automobiles lately? Many of them don't even show a picture of the car. They show other images instead, images that are associated with a happy family, an exciting ride in the mountains, or a peaceful road. Each of these images evokes certain feelings, which the auto manufacturers hope you then associate with the brand of car itself. Thus, if you're shopping for a sporty car, you will more likely buy the one that makes you "feel" sporty rather than the one with the best torque.

When you go home to Mom's house, there are all sorts of all old memories associated with your childhood that are evoked when you visit, which can make you feel nine years old again: your old bedroom, certain foods and cooking smells, the way a certain floorboard creaks when you walk on it. These memories are associated with emotions. Some emotions are pleasant; others are not. Depending on the degree of harmony in your family, you will experience predominantly positive or predominantly negative emotions when you visit your old home. The unpleasant memories and emotions will elicit inner-brat reactions.

The lesson here is this: If you are trying to change your behavior or your reaction to things, it will be more difficult if you don't also modify your environment. It is important to reduce the number of situational cues that have become associated with the habits you're trying to change. The situational cues that trigger old habits also trigger your inner brat's whining and complaining. Think about what happens when you walk past a bakery in the morning. The aroma is irresistible. If your inner brat wasn't thinking about having a cinnamon roll before, it certainly demands one now. By taking a different route in the morning, you don't have to deal with the bakery aroma in the first place, a choice that also helps prevent the emergence of your inner brat.

Bad Moods

When you are depressed or gloomy, you have more difficulty mustering up the energy to deal with your inner brat. It's all you can do to make it through the day. Anxiety and worry make you feel out of control, which is draining in itself. When you are in a bad mood, you expend most of your mental strength in trying to withstand or overcome the mood. Furthermore, most people in a bad mood are extremely self-focused. Such self-focus encourages inner-brat thoughts and makes the bad mood even worse.

"I certainly can't control what kind of mood I'm in," you might say. "These feelings just happen." If you've been reading and paying attention to the ideas in this book, you will dismiss such thoughts. Although you can't totally prevent sadness, worry, anger, or other negative emotions, you can moderate them. Just as you can blow feelings out of proportion by awfulizing and other cognitive distortions, you can bring them back into perspective by using alternative thought processes. These will be described in the next chapter.

Negative moods, such as guilt over having given in to temptation, can lead to cognitive distortions that emphasize failure. For instance, if you have been following your weight-loss program all week and then on Saturday night have cake for dessert, you might feel enormously guilty. Accompanying the guilt might be discouraging thoughts, such as, "I'm a failure ... I can't follow through on this one thing." This state of mind, in turn, changes your expectations of what you should be able to accomplish. If prior to the lapse you had every expectation that you could lose twenty pounds, now you've changed that expectation, such that you won't even bother trying. Your inner brat will have won that round.

Alcohol and Drugs

Even if you don't have a major problem with drinking or illegal drugs, when you use them, they lower your inhibitions. You say and do things that you would not ordinarily do when sober. Drugs and alcohol actually affect the part of the brain that is responsible for judgment and discretion. When your inhibitions are decreased, your inner brat has much more latitude to do harm.

Withdrawal Symptoms

When you try to withdraw from a substance on which you have become dependent, you are apt to suffer physical withdrawal symptoms. If you decide to quit smoking cold turkey, you will experience some jitteriness and other sensations, which are more than just psychological. The same is true for alcohol, caffeine, sugar, and even some medications. The physical symptoms are uncomfortable and command your attention. As pointed out earlier, the discomfort can easily divert your attention from the reason you quit using or ingesting the stuff in the first place. Your inner brat is easily influenced by the withdrawal symptoms. It will cry out in your head, "I can't stand this! Make it go away! Give me my fix [of nicotine, alcohol, caffeine, sugar, etc.]."

All-or-Nothing Thinking

I said earlier that someone who is trying to quit drinking should stay out of bars and not take even a sip of alcohol. This is the ideal situation. However, it's not a good idea to adopt an all-or-nothing approach. If you do, once you take the first sip, you may give up altogether. I have seen people who start exercise programs. They tell themselves, "I'm going to exercise every single day." One day they give in to their inner brat and don't exercise. Now that they've broken the magic of perfection, they often quit exercising completely.

When you start out on a program to make positive changes in your life, you usually intend to stick with it. Of course you don't intend to fail. If you adopt a "zero tolerance" policy, however, you will be vulnerable to giving up your efforts after a single lapse.

Many people believe that absolute adherence to a program is the only way to gain self-control. This was the early philosophy of the diet industry, which fifty years ago gave dieters strict rules about what was allowed and what was forbidden. Guess what? Less than 5 percent of dieters were successful in losing weight and keeping it off. Now programs such as Weight Watchers advertise that there are no forbidden foods. You can choose what you are going to eat. If you have a piece of cake, there are guidelines for making adjustments to compensate. Although the success rate hasn't improved much, these flexible programs attract and keep more clients.

Alcoholics Anonymous (AA) has a zero-tolerance policy. It promotes abstinence as the only answer for someone who has a drinking problem. While this approach works for many people, it may not be necessary for everyone. There are some groups that advocate controlled drinking. Moderation Management is a self-help group for people who want to cut down on their drinking but don't want to eliminate alcohol altogether. Its critics say moderation is not possible. As evidence, they cite the fact that the founder of this group, Audrey Kishline, recently killed a man and his twelve-year-old daughter when she drove while drunk. What they don't tell you is that months before the crash, she had resigned from Moderation Management and gone over to Alcoholics Anonymous, which preaches abstinence. Thus, her fatal accident occurred during a period when drinking was forbidden. I don't know whether her intent was to get drunk that night or not, but her blood-alcohol level was .26, way over the legal limit of intoxication. As an AA member, she may well have resorted to the assumption that she had "blown" her abstinence and so gave up on trying to control her drinking.

An all-or-nothing, zero-tolerance rule almost always sets you up for conflict with your inner brat. Most people don't like to have restrictions. Many arguments over civil rights stem from someone being told he or she can't do something. Some complaints are legitimate, while others are just bratty.

Prisoners serving long sentences are notorious for filing frivolous lawsuits that clog up the courts. These people are already restricted from most of their freedoms. When they feel deprived in addition, they get mad. In Britain, for example, a convict serving a life sentence sued the prison because they wouldn't let him use his money-off coupon to buy a box of cereal. (He won, by the way. The government had to pay him 35 cents plus bear the $900 legal bill.) Another inmate sued when he missed breakfast because of a warden's meeting. In the United States, prisoners have sued for being denied soap on a rope, Rogaine, chunky peanut butter, and more.

Such ridiculous complaints are not limited to prisoners. A couple of years ago, I was on a plane that was flying to a destination about one hour away. Just after takeoff, the flight attendant announced that no peanuts would be served on this flight because one of the passengers had such a bad allergy to peanuts that even the smell of them could set off a potentially fatal reaction. The opposition from the passengers around me was, to put it mildly, militant. They grumbled about being deprived of the snack that they had paid for, and some of them threatened to complain to the authorities about the arbitrary decision that had been made "without warning." You'd think that they were being ordered to sacrifice a limb.

There are thousands of such stories of bratty behavior. What they have in common is that people resent being told "No." This is what Alcoholics Anonymous and other similar programs tell their members. When people set absolute standards for themselves in which error is treated as a major personal felony, they are bound to experience resistance from their inner brat.

Unrealistic Expectations

Unrealistic expectations are related to all-or-nothing thinking. If you set your expectations at an unrealistic level, you will become frustrated. One of the most common examples of this factor occurs among dieters. The media portray the ideal female body as something close to a skeleton with skin. Some models are naturally thin, but most impose severe limits on their food intake in order to stay thin. Many of them continually obsess about food because they are always hungry.

Dieting is a preoccupation in this country. Diet books and weight-loss programs present "before" and "after" pictures of models, implying that you, too, can lose eighty pounds just by drinking some supplement or taking some pills or just by signing up for certain group meetings. It was only recently that a law was passed requiring weight-loss programs to print a disclaimer that the models they present are not typical in their weight loss. In other words, just because you see a picture of somebody who reduced six dress sizes does not mean that you will achieve similar results.

These disclaimers are in very small print. Women still expect that they should be able to wear a size four. It is well documented that only about 5 percent of dieters maintain significant weight loss after five years. While you may be able to lose one or two sizes, if you have always been chubby, it is unlikely that you will ever be rail thin—unless, of course, you get very sick or you make a career of starving yourself.

Exercise is another area where people set unrealistic expectations. You may be familiar with the infomercials on television which promise that, if you buy a certain machine or apparatus, you will have a flat stomach, slim hips, and taut waistline. In thirty days, when you don't achieve the desired results that they promise, you become discouraged and give up altogether. When you become disappointed at not getting the results you expected, you begin to talk to yourself in negative ways. You lose the motivation to keep going. When your inner brat wants a candy bar or when it doesn't feel like getting up and exercising, you are more likely to give in, because, after all, what's the use of trying anyway?

Biological Obstacles against Change

Besides being influenced by physical states, stress, situational cues, and counterproductive mind-sets, we must also come to terms with certain genetic and biological limits on ourselves. Certain aspects of the personality are believed to be inborn, or acquired in the womb or shortly thereafter. The following are some such characteristics that give the inner brat an edge.

Activity Level

People vary in their range of activity. Some are more lively and impulsive. There is strong evidence that impulsivity, at least in part, is genetically determined. Studies of identical twins adopted into separate homes show that, along with other personality traits, their level of impulsiveness is more similar to one another's than to the family members they were raised with. Since identical twins have identical sets of genes, the similarity between them is attributed to heredity.

Here's an example. Let's suppose that you are an identical twin who was adopted into one family and that your twin sibling, whom you don't even know about, was adopted into another family. Let's further assume that you are lively and restless and that your adoptive family is very quiet and sedate. Even though you might love them dearly, you always feel somewhat different from them. If you were to meet your long-lost sibling thirty years later, you would find that, regarding personality, you are more similar to your sibling than to your adoptive family. This similarity includes your level of impulsivity.

If impulsiveness is inherited, does this mean that it is impossible to control it? Not necessarily. Among the twin studies, it has been determined that heredity accounts for only about 50 percent of one's tendency to be impulsive. Environment accounts for the rest. Nevertheless, if you have a habit of being spontaneous, you are one of those people who must learn to pay more attention to the consequences of your behavior and must learn to develop more control.

I hope that this news does not propel your inner brat into action, such that you start whining, "But that's not fair." It's not a matter of fair; it's a matter of human variability. Some people are more impulsive than others, just as some people are taller than others or better "endowed" with larger breasts or penises than others. This is the package you live in, and you have to make the best of it.

Besides, heredity is only partially responsible. Environment and learning also play a role. Even if you are an impulsive individual, you still have choices about how to direct your behavior. Just as a very short-statured person can have a satisfying life, so can a someone with an impulsive nature. And while short people can't do much about their height, impulsive people can learn a few extra adaptational skills. These skills will be discussed in the next chapter.

Keep in mind that not all impulsivity is counterproductive. The core of impulsivity is that of reacting quickly. If you're one of those quick reactors, you probably do well in emergencies. When I evaluate applicants for our local fire department, I look for candidates who don't need to take too much time to deliberate. Imagine an overly cautious firefighter musing to himself about the pros and cons of going into the burning building now as opposed to waiting five minutes or thinking about the best angle at which to hold the hose. This kind of approach may be suitable for a plumber, but in life-or-death situations, I want someone who acts immediately.

Excitability

Another biological factor that can make it more difficult to control your inner brat is your level of physical reactivity or excitability. Some people are naturally calm, while others react more intensely. For example, a person who has low reactivity will not get too upset when he finds his car has a flat tire; neither will he get very excited when he learns that he has received a promotion. On the other hand, an excitable individual reacts to minor frustrations as if they are crises and reacts to good news with exuberant enthusiasm. These variations among people's reactions are not limited to their behavior. It is also seen in physiological responses. An excitable person shows a greater fluctuation in heart rate, sweating, and blood pressure than does someone who is more mellow.

You can probably predict which people have the most trouble with their inner brats—the excitable ones, of course. If you are such an individual, then you will need to monitor your inner brat more closely than will your friends who are what we call "laid-back."

Extroversion

In chapter 8, I described extroverted and introverted personality styles. While the extrovert is more outgoing and talkative, the introvert is pensive and reflective. Extroverts also tend to seek more stimulation. They place themselves in situations where they can react and interact. People who seek stimulation are more apt to take risks and to be spontaneous, especially in social situations. More often than introverts, they tend to say things that they might later regret. In other words, their inner brats are more verbally expressive.

If you are an extrovert, you may need to monitor your inner brat a little more closely when you're angry, lest you say something that you later wish you hadn't. If you are also physically spontaneous, you may need to curb your urges to strike out at people or things.

Implications

In this chapter, you've learned about various obstacles that interfere with effective control of your inner brat. Considering these obstacles as well as the social and cultural influences described earlier, it's not surprising that we haven't been very successful in controlling our inner brats. When self-centered whining and complaining are not only tolerated but sometimes reinforced by society, people don't recognize the benefits of changing their beliefs and behaviors. Even when they do, they become easily discouraged by how difficult it seems.

By minimizing some of the barriers described in this chapter, you will increase your chances of taming your inner brat. You may not be able to eliminate obstacles, but you can manage them. Keep in mind the "Serenity Prayer" by the late Dr. Reinhold Niebuhr:

God, grant me the serenity to
Accept the things I cannot change;
The courage to change the things I can;
And the wisdom to know the difference.

Now that you are armed with "the wisdom to know the difference," let's move to the tools that will help you take charge

12

Strategies for Putting You in Control of Your Inner Brat

You have learned by now that your inner brat is a very powerful force inside you. It is the primitive part of your personality that seeks immediate gratification, no matter what the consequences. You sometimes become so consumed by your inner brat that you get caught up in the impulse of the moment. Your inner brat is like a bratty little child that lives within the depths of your psyche. It wants what it wants, and it wants it right now. Just as a bratty child gets more bratty when adults give in, the more you succumb to your inner brat, the more control it gains over you.

People who are ruled by their inner brats are immature, self-centered, and impulsive. They blame their troubles on other people or situations. They react only to what they want right now or to what is irritating them right now. And many of them feel irritated and victimized much of the time. Who wouldn't when they believe that none of their problems, losses, or pain is ever their fault?

If you find yourself giving in to your inner brat more than you'd like to, you know the feeling of "I wish I hadn't said that" or "I wish I hadn't done that." Even when you tell yourself, "I'll never do it again," you end up doing it again anyway. That's because, like a bratty child, your inner brat doesn't give up easily. Its sole purpose is to satisfy its cravings and urges. Unlike a bratty child, it never grows up. It's with you for life. And while you can walk away from bratty children or put them in time-out, you can't walk away from your inner brat.

Nevertheless, you can push the inner brat to a less prominent place in your mind. You can learn to ignore it, challenge it, and manage it so that it does not control your life. People have said to me, "That's easier said than done." They're right. Taming your inner brat takes work. It takes effort. But it's worth it. If you think about the accomplishments that you are most proud of, they are the ones for which you had to work the hardest. Self-esteem comes from self-exertion.

It's time to stop whining and blaming. You're not a poor victim. You are responsible and accountable for your actions and for every word that leaves your mouth. While you aren't guaranteed a comfortable life, you do have a certain degree of control over how you experience it. Your self-esteem and your relationships with other people can be vastly improved when you take charge of your inner brat.

So, if you're ready to work, here are the tools. Keep in mind that the inner brat is not a physical entity. It is not located anywhere specifically in the brain, nor is it identifiable by brain chemistry. The inner brat is just a shortcut for describing the part of you that is overly self-focused, irrational, and impulsive. The reason for using such a concept is that it helps you see yourself more objectively. Also, you don't have to remember any theories or equations. You already know what a brat is, and now that you know what to look for, it's not that hard to recognize brattiness within yourself.

The Three-Step Process

Taming your inner brat requires three major steps. First, you must calm it down. Next, you must listen to what your inner brat is "saying." Third, you must take charge by applying one or more mental or behavioral strategies. These strategies are based on scientific research. We know they work at least for some people. No strategy works for everyone, and even those that seem to work for you most of the time will not always be effective. Thus, it's best to arm yourself with more than one tool.

Calming

If you've ever tried to reason with a child who's having a tantrum, you know that logic doesn't work very well. At such times, if you try to start a discussion, you just get a shouting match. The same thing happens with your inner brat. It shouts in your mind, drowning out logical arguments.

Consider the example of Gail, a single mother with an eleven-year-old daughter. At each one of her daughter's soccer games, she sees the girl's father in the stands, along with his new wife. Gail has trouble concentrating on the game because she is so angry at him. "How dare he bring that slut to our daughter's game!" she exclaims to herself. From there, Gail's thoughts go back to her marriage and to the affair he was having with the woman who is now his wife. Gail still feels betrayed and hurt. "He has no right to be here," she thinks, "no right at all, after what he's done to us." Every few minutes, Gail interrupts these thoughts. "It's been four years since the separation," she tries to reason. "Just stop this nonsense and get over it." But her inner brat won't get over it. It refuses to let go of the resentment. By the end of the soccer game, Gail is so upset that she doesn't even know what the score was.

Gail's problem here is that she is trying to talk sense to her inner brat, but the inner brat is not rational. Just as it's not very productive to have a rational conversation with an irrational person, it's useless to try to have a rational discussion with your irrational inner brat, especially when it is charged up. In order to get the inner brat to at least listen, you must first calm it down.

Saying things to yourself like "Stop acting so stupid!" or "Quit being so childish!" will not calm you down. If anything, they intensify the negative emotion. Is that how you would talk to a young child who cries because he dropped his ice cream cone or because he couldn't snap his Legos together? You could try yelling at him, "Stop the silly crying," but I guarantee that the child will cry more loudly if you do. A more effective way to deal with that situation would be to say some soothing words first, just to get the child to stop crying. Then you can help him decide what to do about his predicament. In the same way, when your inner brat is acting up, you must first help it calm down.

While talking soothingly helps quiet an upset child, this approach doesn't usually work with your inner brat, at least not right away. What does often calm the inner brat, however, is a simple breathing technique. This technique takes less than a minute to accomplish.

Read the following instructions for deep breathing and then take a minute to try it. It is very important to practice this technique on a regular basis—at least once or twice per day. By doing so, you will have the skill ready when you need it. Consider the practice as training. In a sense, it is. You are training yourself to calm down. The time to practice is when you feel relatively calm already. You need to *overlearn* this skill so that it can be summoned at a moment's notice.

To illustrate how previous practice can come in handy, let me give you an example of my own experience. When I rent a car at the airport, I'm usually eager to get going to my destination, so I try to leave the airport as quickly as possible. One day, while driving a rental car, it started to rain. I reached for the windshield-wiper control, but it wasn't where I expected it. In this rental car, it was in a different place, and it took some fumbling until I found it. On other occasions, I tried to find the volume controls and station buttons for the radio while driving. These maneuvers were not only awkward, but they also distracted me from keeping my eyes and mind on traffic. (I know. It would have been better to pull over to the side of the road. But I was stubborn, and this was before I was aware of my inner brat.) You get the general idea here. If I had familiarized myself with the buttons and levers before I started driving the car, my trip would have been a lot less frustrating. I would have been able to find the controls when I needed them.

Similarly, if you don't practice the breathing technique before you actually need to use it, you will find yourself frantically fumbling around and trying to remember what to do and where to start.

Here are the simple instructions:

1. Sit in a comfortable chair with your eyes closed and your hands in a relaxed position.

2. Inhale slowly to a count of four. Be sure to use all four counts to inhale. Don't gasp to the count of "one" and hold your breath for the other three counts. Allow your chest to expand gradually.

3. Exhale slowly to a count of four. Make your exhaling breath last through all four counts.

4. Count to yourself while you are breathing. Counting will help you focus your mind on your body. Getting into the habit of counting one...two...three...four...will help distract you from competing, negative thoughts later on, and it will help drown out inner-brat whining in the back of your mind.

5. Repeat the inhale/exhale sequence three more times.

As you master this exercise, you will notice a definite slowing down of racing thoughts and physical symptoms of anxiety or anger. You will feel more focused and centered. This technique is similar to that used by world-class athletes before a competition, by top-notch actors and other performers who get stage fright, and by others who must quickly gain mental focus.

After practicing once or twice per day, you will be ready when your inner brat emerges. When you feel suddenly angry or impatient or when you find yourself tempted by something you promised to avoid, just stop and breathe. At that point, you don't even need to find a comfortable chair.

The important thing is to take a minute to calm yourself. I know that inner brats can seem urgent and persistent, but even the most obnoxious inner brat can wait one more minute.

Listening

The next step is to listen carefully to what your inner brat is saying or implying. It may not be talking to you in actual words, but the message is usually pretty clear. Most people don't stop to think about the message; they reflexively act on impulse, which is precisely what the inner brat wants.

In order to listen to what your inner brat is saying, it may be necessary to translate feelings and impressions into words. For example, when someone passes a candy dish to you, you may take a candy without thinking. But if you stop to analyze what prompted you to take a candy, you will notice a sequence of events:

1. The candy dish is passed to you. The appearance of the candy dish is a situational cue.

2. Your notice the candy.

3. The candy looks good.

4. You recognize that, on some level, you want some.

5. Your brain directs your hand to reach for a candy and pop it into your mouth.

All of these steps usually take less than a second or two. You're probably not even aware of the sequence of thoughts and movements. However, when you stop to think about what you're doing, your inner brat is no longer automatically in control. Of course, neither is your rational self automatically in control, either. In fact, while you look at the candy, you might have a moment of hesitation when the dish is passed to you. You might have the little argument going on in your head: "I want it . . . but I shouldn't . . . but it looks really good . . ." At that point, you are more aware of your inner brat's manipulations. It is the voice calling, "I want it." If you say "No," it might resort to rationalization, such as, "Go ahead. You skipped dessert at lunch."

Whether or not you're aware of the ideas floating around in your mind, they are there. When you learn to pay attention to them, you can better understand them. Also, the sooner you pay attention the better, because, as noted in the last chapter, the deeper you are into a self-defeating sequence of thought or behavior, the harder it is to stop. Thus, the moment you pick up a candy from the dish, you increase the chance that you will eat it—and perhaps several more as well.

Once you become aware of your inner brat's presence, the next step is to figure out what it's saying. It may be using the simple nagging technique of "I want it." Or perhaps it's using one of the cognitive distortions discussed in chapter 9. It is also quite possible that your inner brat is assuming that something or someone "must" behave in the way you want; or perhaps it is magnifying the negative impact of a situation. All-or-nothing thinking, magnification, dwelling on the negative, generalizing from a single instance, emotional reasoning, and fortune-telling are other cognitive distortions that your inner brat uses. Your inner brat may also adopt manipulative personae, as described in chapter 8. Your inner brat, which represents self-centered, irrational impulses, will use whatever it takes to satisfy its urges and relieve its angry tension.

If this seems like a lot to pay attention to, it's not surprising. Your inner brat exists at the core of your personality. It has pervasive influence in many areas of your life. You have built up years of rationalizations and other cognitive distortions. You've developed a habit of acting and saying certain things without considering the consequences. This complex array is the product of your inner brat.

As indicated earlier, it's going to take work to regain control over your inner brat. But with practice, the work will not be so strenuous. Think back to the time when you first learned to drive. Remember all the things you had to remember? For example, when you saw a light turn red up ahead, you had to begin braking early. You also had to make sure you kept a safe distance from the car in front of you. If you learned to drive using a stick shift, you had to remember to step on the clutch and shift gears all at the same time. The early stages of learning to drive can be quite taxing. Today, however, you don't consciously think of all those steps. You just do them. It's much less effort to drive now than it was when you were just learning. The same goes for learning to manage your inner brat. While it seems like a lot of work now, with practice you will be able to do it more or less automatically.

Taking Charge

Taking charge of your inner brat is similar to gaining control over a situation with a bratty child. Yelling, threatening, and arguing might work for the moment, but these approaches don't prevent future bratty outbursts.

Recall from the last chapter that the more you try to suppress thoughts, the stronger they seem to become, such that it's increasingly difficult to get them out of your mind. In the same way, the more you try to tell your inner brat to "shut up," the more intensely it complains.

When the inner brat is first active, it does not usually have total control. The inner brat, which represents your narcissistic, irrational self, is often in contention with your rational self. This conflict is especially evident when you're trying to resist temptation. If you pay close attention to the conversation of ideas floating around in your mind, you'll probably notice that there is a power struggle. If you've ever been in a power struggle with a whiny or undisciplined child, you know how draining that can be. It is the same with your inner brat. Internal arguments or other attempts to oppose it will not eliminate the power struggle. You'll be so worn down that the inner brat will eventually win.

The best way to take charge of your inner brat is with a gentle but firm approach. Here are some suggestions, starting with what *not* to do:

- **Don't get into an argument with your inner brat.** Don't mull over the pros and cons. The longer you keep your inner brat engaged in debate, the greater the chance that it will find a way to get you to give in.

- **Don't dwell on visualizing what your inner brat says it wants or needs.** This advice applies not only to food, tobacco, alcohol, or drugs but also to material things that it claims it must have. If your inner brat is focused on thoughts of jealousy or envy, do not spend time imagining scenarios that will only make you feel worse.

- **Don't treat your inner brat as an equal.** It is not your equal. You don't have to listen to its every word or thought. Many people think that once they start dwelling on something, they must finish the thought. You don't have to. You can quit in the middle.

- **Don't always trust your feelings.** While "Trust your feelings" was the slogan of pop psychology during the past three decades, it was not very effective. Your inner brat is highly emotional and impulsive. Trusting your feelings when dealing with matters of temptation, revenge, and procrastination only gives your inner brat permission to carry out its primitive wishes.

And here's what you *should* do to minimize conditions under which the inner brat thrives:

- **Do get plenty of sleep.** Remember, fatigue is one of the most common reasons for losing control. Don't underestimate the power of being well-rested.

- **Do try to minimize stress.** You read in the last chapter that stress depletes your resources to cope in general. Keep situational stress to a minimum. Commit yourself only to what is necessary. Avoid making extra work for yourself. Learn to say "no" to people who take advantage of you. Keep internal stress to a minimum. When you find yourself brooding or dwelling on something, remind yourself that you have limited mental resources. I tell my clients to pretend that they have a dollar's worth of energy to spend during a day. When they start dwelling on resentments and other negative thoughts, I ask them if it's worth spending fifty cents on those thoughts or if they'd rather save the energy for something more beneficial.

- **Do make changes in your environment.** Recall that situational cues can trigger inner-brat thoughts, feelings, and behaviors. Therefore, if you want to lose weight, keeping tempting foods out of the house isn't enough. You must also change your routines for eating, including the time and the place. For example, if you're accustomed to eating in front of the television, change where you sit, or better yet, don't watch television. Avoid walking into the kitchen. If you're tempted by alcohol, don't visit bars. If you want to spend less money, leave your credit cards at home and carry only the cash you intend to spend. If you find yourself playing computer games when you should be working, remove the games from the computer. These are a few examples of how you can set up your environment to help prevent your inner brat from sabotaging your efforts.

- **Do avoid alcohol and stimulants.** Alcohol interferes with self-control, and stimulants can make you more irritable. These give your inner brat the edge, especially if you have problems with anger and frustration.

- **Do have a specific plan, not only for the goal you aim for but also for how and when you're going to do it.** Research shows that you have a much better chance of success at reaching a goal if you have a specific plan. Visualize yourself doing these things at a time when your inner brat is not in the foreground. Stick to your plan regardless of how you feel.

- **Do provide external reminders to keep your goal in perspective.** As an external reminder, some people put a picture of a fat person on the refrigerator to remind them how they don't want to look. (Other people put up a picture of a thin person to remind them of how they do want to look.) In this way, when their inner brat demands ice cream, the picture on the fridge gives them a chance to hesitate before opening the freezer door.

- **Do give your inner brat a name.** Some people think that naming the brat is silly because there is no such entity as an inner brat. "Besides," they sometimes ask, "won't that turn me into a split personality?" No, it won't. The purpose of giving your inner brat a name is to designate it as something separate from your true "self." Do you recall that earlier I explained how individuals resist acknowledging their own shortcomings but can easily spot them in other people? When you give your inner brat a name, it's almost as if you can pretend it's another person. Because it is regarded as less central to your core self, it is easier to view your problems objectively and to deal with them effectively.

Intervention: What to Do

First, remember that *you* are ultimately in charge, not your inner brat. If your immediate survival depended on resisting temptation or holding your tongue, you would not give in to your inner brat's demands. Although resisting your inner brat depletes you of mental energy, resisting doesn't drain your energy completely. There is always a little in reserve. Don't forget this. Overriding your inner brat's impulse by exercising control over your behavior will ultimately build up your mental strength in the same way that physical exercise builds up physical strength. In the future, therefore, you will expend less effort to accomplish the same end.

- **Do treat your inner brat as you would a bratty child.** Instead of arguing, make a decision and start acting on it immediately. Think what happens when you tell a bratty child, "Stop it. I really mean it this time," but you don't follow through. As soon as you are aware of your inner brat's manipulation, do something immediately to show you mean business. This action will take energy, but you won't regret exerting yourself.

- **Do visualize your inner brat as a bratty, cartoon-like child.** This will help emphasize the fact that your inner brat is not some all-powerful mysterious force but merely an immature little imp that needs to be reigned in.

- **Do keep a realistic perspective.** Pace yourself. Your inner brat wants what it wants, and it wants it now. You are not at its mercy. Remember: *You* decide what to do and when. *You* are in charge. Announce that it must wait a few minutes. A realistic perspective implies objectivity. Although it is hard to be objective when your inner brat is vying for control, there are some things you can do. For example, remind yourself that if you are upset, it is quite possible that you have a distorted view of the facts. Also, review the situation that is upsetting you, but this time, pay attention to as many details as you can. Say them out loud or write them down. This will force you to notice factors that you might have missed previously, and that might help put the situation into a more realistic perpective.

- **Do distract yourself from your inner brat, once you've calmed it down.** By distraction I mean that you shouldn't just try to let your mind wander but, rather, find something specific to do or think about that engages your attention. Research shows that when your attention is actively involved in something that you enjoy or find challenging, you do not have as much of a "rebound effect." In other words, don't just actively try to ignore the inner brat, because this attempt only depletes your mental strength. Instead, distract yourself. There is a better chance that your inner brat's complaining will fade.

- **Do apply discipline to your inner brat.** Discipline is not the same as punishment or deprivation. The actual meaning of discipline is "training that develops self-control." Children, including bratty ones, feel secure with limits, even though they test them periodically. They respond well to a clear sense of just how far they can go. Your inner brat will also test limits. But if you are consistent, you can train children, and likewise, you can train your inner brat to protest less.

- **Do be persistent and consistent.** Bratty children do not change their tactics after a single confrontation. It often takes several "lessons" for the bratty child to learn to comply. In the same way, it will take many interventions for you to get your inner brat under control. Given the fact that your inner brat may be thirty, forty, fifty years old or more, that's a long record of old habits to revise. Be careful not to allow too many "just this once" exceptions. In fact, in the beginning stages, it's best to be rigidly consistent, at least for a week. If you aren't strict, your inner brat will get the idea that if it complains loudly enough and long enough, it will get its own way and consequently will escalate its efforts. Unless you are persistent and consistent, you will end up with an inner brat that is more unmanageable than previously.

- **Do set contingencies for your inner brat.** The basic premise is to complete a less desirable activity in order to earn a more desirable activity. Just as you would say to a child, "You can watch television *after* you've done your homework, you can say to your inner brat, "After you work on the bills, you can read your magazine." This "work before play" approach works especially well with a brat who likes to procrastinate.

Intervention: What to Tell Your Inner Brat

In the preceding section are listed behavioral techniques that are effective in dealing with a bratty child—and also with your inner brat. Next are strategies for talking to yourself and your inner brat.

- **Do use humor.** Humor helps deflate the intensity of the inner brat's force. Suppose, for example, that you're driving behind a slowpoke and you can't change lanes. As the tension builds, first calm yourself. Then pay attention to the irrational statements that the inner brat is uttering, such as, "This is awful. It's terrible." Rather than dispute that belief, try saying to yourself, "Yes, this is the worst thing that ever happened to anyone. I'll never get over this." Such humorous exaggeration will put the situation into perspective.

- **Do ask yourself, "Will this matter in a week? Will it even matter in an hour?"** This approach also puts things into perspective so that you don't have to view them as so urgent. It works especially well in situations that are temporarily frustrating, such as waiting in line, getting cut off on the telephone, or dealing with angry people. Remember, just because something feels urgent doesn't mean necessarily that it's important.

- **Do take on a parental role with your inner brat.** Just because your inner brat gets upset, angry, bitchy, or whiny, you don't have to respond to its every complaint. In fact, a highly effective technique is not to discuss the complaint at all. For example, when your inner brat whines that it must get its own way, you can acknowledge that fact, but say, "This is what I decided when I was rational. It's non-negotiable now." And keep repeating that to yourself.

- **Do make a decision.** Decide not only what you *will* do about the situation but also what you *will not do*. This commitment is especially useful for the inner brat that gets angry and for the inner brat that procrastinates. Once you decide what you're not going to do, you'll experience a sense of relief. You can then focus your attention on a shorter list of options, which is much less overwhelming.

- **Do remember that you are stronger than your inner brat.** There is almost no urge that is absolutely impossible to resist. Even coughing, which we assume is a physical reflex, can be suppressed when necessary. If you've ever attended a symphony, you may have noticed that, while the orchestra is playing, people don't cough much. But when the music stops, there is a round of coughing throughout the auditorium. The same thing happens at plays and lectures. When you think that your inner brat has a strong grip on you, remember this example. You are in charge, and you should say so to your inner brat.

- **Do make statements that cut the problem down to size.** This approach usually works only after you have successfully calmed your inner brat down. Saying things such as, "It's only for a couple of minutes," "This isn't the first time that you've had to do that," or "You're almost halfway there" helps put the problem into perspective and adds an encouraging message. Years ago, I used to be terrified of the dentist and of the hygienist as well, and I put on quite a fearful display in the chair. One day I had a new hygienist. She did not indulge my self-pitying drama. Instead, she looked me in the eye and said, "You know, there's not much to this. You've given birth. That's a lot worse than getting your teeth cleaned." Since then, I've been much less of a brat at the dentist's office.

- **Do ask yourself, "What's the worst thing that can happen?"** Until you articulate that question to yourself, you just have a vague feeling that something terrible will happen, something that you won't be able to handle. Once you specify the worst-case scenario, you can then decide on a plan of action. For example, if your children are dawdling on Sunday morning and you're running late for church, is it necessary to yell at them? What's the worst thing that can happen? You'll walk in late. People will stare. You will feel conspicuous. That's it—not pleasant, but not fatal either. A few years ago (when my knees still worked well), I planned to run a 10K race. This race required advance registration, which caused me some concern, because there was a chance of rain on the day of the race. As I plunked down my application form and ten dollars, I asked the woman, "What happens if it rains?" She rolled her eyes, looked at me with disdain, and said curtly, "You'll get wet." Of course I *knew* that, but once it was articulated to me, it didn't seem all that bad. Adopting an attitude of "It's not such a big deal" takes power away from your inner brat.

- **Do look for solutions instead of whining about problems.** When you focus on solutions, you feel more empowered and can better anticipate a sense of closure. Instead of feeling sorry for yourself and dwelling on your anger toward someone else, ask yourself, "What are my options? What can I do now?" Make a plan. Say it to yourself, or better yet, write it down. For example, suppose you applied for a job that you really wanted, but you did not get hired. In such a situation, it would be very easy for you to dwell on your disappointment, courtesy of your inner brat. On the other hand, such a negative fixation won't bring you any closer to finding satisfying employment. What are your options? What can you do?

Once you start shifting your focus to planning the future, you will feel more optimistic and less victimized. A focus on solutions helps you deal with many different types of situations, including frustration, long-term resentment, failure of any kind, jealousy, and envy. By thinking of options and planning specific courses of action, you may not eradicate your negative feelings, but you can certainly lessen them.

These suggestions highlight what you can do to take charge of your inner brat. The general message is this: Don't make mountains out of molehills. Make molehills out of mountains.

Troubleshooting

Now let's address the subject of attitude and expectations. As indicated earlier, it will take time to feel more in control. It will also be uncomfortable at times. Be prepared to tolerate a higher level of frustration and anxiety. When children are subject to a change of rules in the home, they put up a fuss, which can be quite disconcerting. If the parents give in during this phase, they inadvertently teach their children that if they whine loudly and long enough, they can get their own way. Thus, the very behavior that the parents are trying to minimize is actually increased.

When you change the rules for your inner brat, it will also try to challenge you. Your discomfort, anger, and other negative feelings might initially get worse. But it's only for a little while. It is very important to ride this phase out. Your inner brat, which is very focused on immediate gratification, does not care about the long-term advantage of maintaining self-control. But *you* do care, and in order to achieve long-term benefit, you often have to put up with short-term discomfort. (Just as my mother used to tell me when she combed snags out my long hair when I was a little girl, "If you want to be beautiful, you have to suffer.") Don't fall into the trap of letting your inner brat complain, "I can't stand this." You may not like it, but you can certainly stand it.

One way to "stand it" is to interpret your discomfort as something useful. For example, if you are trying to lose weight and you have hunger pangs, you don't need to say to yourself, "I'm so very, very hungry." Instead, try saying, "Good, my stomach's empty. That means my body has to start burning fat." If you feel your anger building up, consider it a challenge rather than an overwhelming impulse. Focus on meeting the challenge. If you crave a cigarette, welcome those withdrawal symptoms. They signify that your body is cleansing itself.

Cognitive Restructuring

The foregoing strategies comprise a process called *cognitive restructuring*. It involves looking at problems from a different angle. This process is exemplified in the old story about the optimist and the pessimist, each in a prison cell with a pile of horse manure in the corner. On his daily rounds, the guard would see the pessimist sitting in the far corner with a piece of cloth covering his nose and mouth to keep out the stench. But whenever he passed the optimist's cell, he noticed the prisoner digging through the manure with his hands. By the third day, the guard could no longer contain his curiosity. When he reached the optimist's cell, he asked, "Why do you keep digging in that manure?" The optimist, too busy to turn around, called out over his shoulder, "With all this crap, there's gotta be a pony in here somewhere!" Thus, even the most vile of circumstances can have a positive implication if you dig far enough.

The main outcome of cognitive restructuring is that it disarms your inner brat. It takes away the urgency, the demandingness of your deeper, irrational self. When you stop interpreting situations and events as awful and terrible, your inner brat retreats into the background of your mind. You may still detect its presence, but at that point it will have very little power. The situations will now be merely uncomfortable, inconvenient, disappointing, or irritating. And those feelings aren't so hard to tackle.

Will This Process Be Worth All the Work?

You have to decide the value of taming your inner brat. It does take effort to change, and you don't usually see the results right away. But do you honestly know anyone who ever regretted taking control, becoming more disciplined and less angry? The more you practice taking charge of your inner brat, the more emotionally resilient you'll become. Little things won't upset you. You'll be more optimistic and better able to bounce back from adversity.

Daniel Goleman, in his 1997 book *Emotional Intelligence,* lists the social and emotional skills that contribute to success in one's work, family life, and other relationships. Among these are

- Being aware of your feelings as they occur.

- Handling distressing emotions in appropriate ways.

- Motivating yourself toward achievement by delaying gratification and stifling impulses.

- Empathy (being able to take other people's perspectives).

- Social skills.[20]

When you take charge of your inner brat, you will also master these tasks. Although Goleman assumes that you are at a permanent disadvantage if you haven't developed these skills by adolescence, other researchers have shown that it is indeed possible to teach an old dog new tricks.

What about Setbacks?

Nobody is 100 percent successful at controlling impulses. Even the most mild-mannered people have inappropriate outbursts. Even the most disciplined among us will blow off an evening of study or will do something that we later regret. Expect an occasional setback, but don't allow that to be your excuse to give up. Giving up is only your inner brat whispering, "See? I told you it was too hard. Now back off and give me what I want." Your inner brat may win a few rounds, but it need not dominate the game.

Adjust Your Expectations

As a product of contemporary society, you are probably influenced by the sense of entitlement that is prevalent today. It is very unhealthy to buy into the notion that you are owed something, because this notion makes you overly self-centered and leaves you feeling at others' mercy. It also places you at risk for feeling like a victim.

Here is an excerpt from the "Bill of No Rights" written by Lewis W. Napper in protest of the American public's demanding more and more services and entitlements from the government:

ARTICLE I

You do not have the right to a new car, big-screen color TV or any other form of wealth. More power to you if you can legally acquire them, but no one is guaranteeing anything.

ARTICLE II

You do not have the right to never be offended. This country is based on freedom, and that means freedom for everyone—not just you! You may leave the room, turn the channel, express a different opinion, etc., but the world is full of idiots, and probably always will be.

ARTICLE III

You do not have the right to be free from harm. If you stick a screwdriver in your eye, learn to be more careful. Do not expect the tool manufacturer to make you and all of your relatives independently wealthy.

The entire ten articles of Napper's "Bill of No Rights" can be viewed at his Web site, www.bServer.com. This document has circled the Internet dozens of times. People are beginning to recognize that rampant narcissism and a sense of entitlement threaten our common sensibility.

You can't change the brattiness of other people, but you do have control over your own bratty thoughts, feelings, and behaviors. You now know what causes them, what sets them off, how to identify them, and what to do about them.

In the next chapter, you will find some examples of how to deal with specific personal problems.

13

Sample Solutions for Specific Problems with Your Inner Brat

T his chapter addresses some typical circumstances in which the inner brat tries to take control. For each situation, I describe how the inner brat might be involved and then suggest some solutions. These are based on the preceding chapters. If you haven't read the book in sequence up to this point, some of the terms and concepts might be unfamiliar. Nevertheless, you should be able to get the gist of what I'm saying.

The following is not a comprehensive self-help program. The descriptions are not diagnoses. As mentioned earlier, if you have constant trouble just getting through the day, then you probably need more help than this book can provide and should contact a mental-health professional. If you need assistance in getting a referral, call the American Psychological Association's "Talk to Someone Who Can Help" line (1-800-964-2000, United States and Canada only), and they will refer you to a psychologist in your area. If you do not live in the United States or Canada, contact your national psychological association or local mental-health facility.

Some of the following recommendations may work for you better than others. You may discover strategies of your own that aren't mentioned in this book. I hope that the suggestions get you thinking creatively so that you can apply the basic principles to your own unique circumstances. It may also be helpful to reread the previous sections that apply to the examples below.

Addictive Behaviors

Addictive behaviors include not only abuse of alcohol, drugs, and tobacco but also gambling, overeating, compulsive shopping, obsessive preoccupation with sex, spending too much time on the Internet, and so on. I am not too concerned here with the clinical definition of addiction, which itself is controversial. If your life is adversely affected by any of these things, then it's a problem you need to deal with.

When people try to overcome their addictions, they encounter a battle of the wills. One part of them wants to stop, while another part cries out for the substance or addictive behavior. This second part, of course, is the inner brat. It demands immediate gratification, while the rational self tries to maintain a steady course toward long-term goals.

If your inner brat is out of control in this sphere, you are dealing not only with physical cravings but also with deeply entrenched habits that are set off by a number of situational cues. These factors make the inner brat quite difficult to manage. As indicated in chapter 11, resisting this type of inner brat depletes you of mental strength. Nevertheless, the depletion is temporary, and with practice, strength increases, just like a muscle that is regularly exercised.

It is most important, when dealing with this kind of inner brat, to approach it as a top priority. Thus, if you want to lose weight, quit smoking, stop drinking, or restrict shopping, you must be prepared to approach it like a regular, part-time job. You don't have to be thinking about it every minute, but you do need to stay vigilant for your inner brat's manipulations. (Review chapter 10 for clues that your inner brat is gaining control. See chapter 11 to remind yourself of the conditions that enhance your inner brat, and take steps to minimize these conditions, especially fatigue, stress, and environmental cues.)

Whenever you are tempted, stall yourself as long as possible in order to give your reasoning power a chance to kick in. Remember to reinterpret your discomfort as something beneficial. Transform "I can't stand it" statements to "Nobody ever died from being deprived of a cigarette (or a brownie, or sex, or a blackjack game)." Think of your inner brat as a persistent pest. Commit yourself to concentrating on something else for only fifteen minutes. Chances are the inner brat will settle down.

Anger

Not all anger is bad. Anger is an emotion that has biological usefulness in human history. It is the emotion that propels people to defend themselves against physical attacks and to fight injustice on behalf of others. But there is a dark side to anger as well. Chronic anger is associated with health problems such as high blood pressure, elevated cholesterol, and weakened immune systems. Anger also interferes with the ability to concentrate, not to mention the toll it takes on your patience and on your relationships with others.

Not all anger is related to the inner brat. There certainly are situations where anger is justified, such as when you have been betrayed or attacked. Not all anger is intense, either. Think of anger not as an all-or-nothing phenomenon but as a range of feelings on a continuum from mild annoyance at one extreme to rage at the other. The inner brat emerges when one of your "emotional hot buttons" (described in chapter 1) is triggered.

The inner brat is involved when you become outraged at something that objectively is only mildly or temporarily irritating. The increasing incidence of road rage involves this type of anger. Road rage has been getting a lot of publicity lately, as if it's a "new" problem in our fast-paced world. It's not a new problem at all. Road rage is just another type of temper tantrum, albeit a potentially lethal one, and temper tantrums have been around since caveman days. They range from having a "short fuse" and lashing out verbally to prolonged shouting matches that may also include physical harm or destruction of property. You may recognize this as the "Eruptor" inner brat (described in chapter 8.)

If you don't have tantrums, perhaps you spend a lot of time sulking and fuming. This behavior, as you learned earlier, is a passive-aggressive form of anger and is more the "Smolderer" type. It can do just as much damage to a relationship as angry outbursts. Although tantrum behavior is intense, it doesn't last very long. Passive-aggressive sulking, on the other hand, can go on for days, weeks, or months. I know couples who avoid talking to each other for weeks because one of them is "punishing" the other. Tantrums, however, are no better than long, drawn-out cold wars. Both forms of expressing anger are destructive.

If any of these descriptions sound like you, there are two possibilities: First, your brain and body may be more reactive in general, such that you feel things more intensely. Second, you have not developed the skills to manage frustration. Naturally, if you have both these factors working against you, you may have to work a little harder at self-control than someone who doesn't have the physical predisposition. But that's just the way it is. You inner brat will need extra-heavy management. (But remember, self-esteem comes from hard work.)

When your inner brat gets angry, your whole body reacts. Physical alertness increases as adrenaline and other hormones start pumping. You feel compelled to do something. Given your state of mind at that time, it's best to wait at least a few minutes. At this point, you can do some calming breathing. Deep breathing will slow down the physical sensations of anger. Remember to count slowly to four as you inhale and to four as you exhale. Counting will help you focus away from what you're angry about. Don't expect to be completely calm at this point. That would be impossible. What you want to aim for is just to "apply the brakes" so that you can figure out what to do next.

After you calm yourself a little, listen to what your inner brat is saying. As with the addictive problems described earlier, this inner brat may also be saying a form of "I can't stand it." But probably stronger are thoughts concerning the way things "should" or "shouldn't" be. Another common inner-brat whine is "That's not fair." If you don't take charge of your inner brat at this point, you're liable to say or do something impulsive, something that you'll later regret.

Don't ignore your anger or pretend it's not there. If you try to do so, you'll have an additional set of problems to deal with. It is not unhealthy to experience anger, but some ways of dealing with it are unhealthy. I'm not referring here to the psychoanalytic notion that if you don't release your anger, it will accumulate and build up until you become a walking time bomb. This theory has never been proven. What does contribute to eruptions is your tendency to dwell on what upset you, to keep it alive in your mind, and to magnify its intensity by making mountains out of molehills.

As for people who claim, "Sure, I have a bad temper, but once I get it out, I'm over it"—well, *they* may be over it, but others around them certainly aren't. If you're one of these people, don't try to undo the damage by saying, "It's my hormones" or "I don't know what got into me." By now, you know that such excuses are just your inner brat trying to avoid responsibility. It's best to acknowledge what you said or did and vow to work at preventing future incidents.

If you have a problem with anger, the good news is that you will have many opportunities to practice self-control. Once you've calmed yourself a little and examined the kinds of irrational statements and complaints that your inner brat is making, there are a number of things you can do. Useful strategies include asking yourself if this will matter in a week as well as anticipating the worst-case scenario. Humor might help if you're not too worked up physically. If at all possible, make a decision to do nothing for a while. This pause will help prevent regret later on. Postponing your reaction may mean that you miss a great opportunity to tell someone off at the right moment, but if the person is that much of a pest, you will have other chances to do so in the future. One way to get out of the rut of dwelling on the injustice that befell you is to create a plan. Make a decision about what you are going to do and also about what you are *not* going to do. While this decision may not solve the problem, it will bring some closure.

Remember, think of your anger as a little brat having a tantrum. Whatever is effective in handling a real-life bratty child will also work on your inner brat. The important thing to remember is that *you* are in charge, not the brat.

There is an expression, "Don't get angry; get even." Although this expression implies that you shouldn't act on impulse, I don't recommend getting even, because plotting your revenge is only going to use up emotional and mental resources that you could better spend on something else. However, when you stop to think before your act impulsively, it keeps your options open and gives you time for your rational self to take over.

Try these techniques for a month. If you find that, even with close monitoring of your inner brat, you feel as if you've made no progress, you may need some professional guidance. Some people find certain medications useful, but medication helps mainly with the calming part. Counseling in addition helps you learn new skills to manage your anger more effectively.

"Poor Me"

Feeling sorry for yourself reflects your inner brat at its victimized best. When you feel like a victim, you essentially absolve yourself of responsibility for what happens to you. But this attitude also implies that you assume life is beyond your control. Being a victim places you in a vicious cycle. You hate what's happening to you, but you don't think there is anything you can do about it—a view that makes you feel even more despondent and resentful.

Self-victimizing thoughts include jealousy, envy, and self-pity as well as martyr-like feelings. When your inner brat engages in such thinking, you dwell on the negative, on what you *don't* have or *can't* do. You feel unworthy and unappreciated. When you get stuck in this frame of mind, you will tend to reject helpful suggestions, even if they make sense.

In contrast to counterproductive anger, which has the effect of making you feel agitated, "poor me" thoughts leave you feeling drained. Therefore, the calming technique is not as critical for slowing down your bodily symptoms, but it does help cool things off in your mind. When you start feeling victimized, don't chastise yourself for being silly or unreasonable. As pointed out earlier, such an approach does not work. Instead, talk soothingly to yourself.

Next, listen to what your inner brat is saying. You may assume that your internal conversations are about the person whom you resent. But if you pay closer attention, you'll probably discern that the conversations are more about you and what you're supposedly lacking. It won't help to focus on what the other guy has that you don't. You can always find people who have more than you or less than you. The ones with more aren't necessarily happier, and the ones with less aren't necessarily more miserable. It is not external events that make you feel the way you do. It's how you interpret them.

For example, suppose Dennis is quite content with his salary. Then he learns that Lorraine, who joined the company around the same time he did, earns a few thousand dollars more, mostly from bonuses. Suddenly Dennis is no longer satisfied with his salary; he feels cheated. What happened here? Prior to his knowledge about Lorraine's income, Dennis believed that he was compensated fairly. Now that he's learned of the discrepancy between the two salaries, he interprets his own paycheck in a different, negative way. Even though his hours and duties remain the same, suddenly he is dissatisfied. He creates his own misery by the way he thinks about the situation.

Let's examine what Dennis's inner brat is saying to him. First, it is complaining that things aren't fair, that he is entitled to more money, because he spends just as much time at work as Lorraine does—even more, because he sometimes has to go in on Saturdays to catch up. Next, his inner brat whines about all the sacrifices he's made for the company, and look where it got him: nowhere, according to his inner brat. This reflection throws Dennis into a despondent mood. And he will stay there as long as he dwells on what he's "entitled" to.

If you, like Dennis, get into the rut of feeling entitled, you will miss the whole point of feeling successful. Success depends on your criteria. If a movie makes $40 million, does that mean it's a success? Financially speaking, yes. But does that mean it's a great movie? That depends. If the film is geared to a teenage audience and you are well into middle age, then you might not deem the movie so wonderful. On the other hand, a less financially profitable film with a cast and story line that appeals to you is what you would define as successful.

Similarly, when you start evaluating your own success, consider which criteria are important. In the work world, is it money, prestige, flexibility, or other factors? In your personal relationships, do you judge success by the number of friends you have, by the occupation of your spouse, or by the accomplishments of your children? Or do you consider success in terms of how you would like to be remembered? Depending on your criteria, you can be content, or you can be miserable.

In this competitive society, there is always a tendency to compare oneself. Competition is the essence of sports, where accomplishments can be measured in terms of scores, speed, and distance. These are all objectively defined units. How do we know that Tiger Woods is a good golfer? To me, his swing looks about the same as other pros' swings. I know he's good because his scores tell me so. But life doesn't usually have such simple measures of success. It's more than statistics. When you start comparing yourself with people on a single dimension, sooner or later you'll feel either resentful or insecure.

Resentment and insecurity get your inner brat into the mind-set of whining and blaming others. You'll end up investing so much energy in feeling victimized that there will be little left for constructive thinking. Therefore, when you start feeling like a victim and your inner brat starts whining, focus on making a plan. You probably have more options than you realize. For example, if you don't like your job, you can either learn to like aspects of it, or you can change jobs altogether. If for one reason or another you feel you can't change your job, think again. Is it really that impossible, or are you not willing to take a pay cut or other risks? Let's say that you decide it's really impossible to get another job. In that case, you're stuck. Figure out what you can do to minimize the job's negative impact. Most likely it will involve changing some of your assumptions and expectations. To bring this new perspective into focus, you may benefit from a few sessions with a therapist, who can help you identify external and internal sources of stress as well as what to do about them.

Self-Defeating Failure to Act

Self-defeating tendencies occur in situations where the emphasis is not on stopping ourselves from doing something but on making ourselves do things that we know are ultimately beneficial. The most common example is procrastination. We know that there's a particular task we should do, but somehow we never get around to it until the last minute, if at all. One reason we procrastinate is because of anxiety. When we anticipate starting a major task, we worry at the back of our minds about whether we can do a good job. When we promise ourselves that we'll start tomorrow, we're absolved of our obligation for now, so we feel some relief. This cycle gets repeated over and over. (For more about procrastination, see chapter 2.) Another reason we procrastinate is because our inner brat does not like to exert itself. Since it's pleasure-oriented, it tries to avoid anything tedious, difficult, or complicated. In terms of the behavior probabilities (described in chapter 11), work is low on the hierarchy for the inner brat. When it's time to study, to work on your income-tax return, to repair a loose doorknob, or to do some other non-fun task, your inner brat will try to convince you to do something else instead.

When the inner brat tries to take over, here's what to do. Above all, do *not* get into any sort of negotiation with your inner brat. That means no promising to do it later, no bargaining for more time, no waiting until you're "in the mood." The fact that you considered getting to your task now means that you know it has to be done and that you could certainly find the time to do it if you absolutely had to. (As proof, don't you always find the time when the deadline is staring you in the face?)

Next, remind yourself who is in charge: *You* are, not your inner brat. So then *act* as if you're in charge. Are you going to be pushed around by a little brat? Only if you decide so. Once you're committed to getting started, expect to experience a little hesitation or anxiety, especially with a major task. This hesitation is normal; it reflects uncertainty about being able to do the job well. In fact, this doubt is the reason you have been avoiding the task in the first place.

If you can't disregard discomfort, use cognitive restructuring to put a less negative spin on it. For example, you might say to yourself, "Of course I don't feel like doing it. If I did, it would have been finished by now. If I avoid it again, I'll regret it later. No matter how hard it is, I certainly won't regret having given it a try." Then commit yourself to working on it for fifteen minutes. You'll probably find that within a few minutes of getting started, your anxiety subsides, and you can keep going for another fifteen minutes, and so on.

For both complex and simple tasks (such as putting something away, sewing on a button, making a telephone call, etc.), you can use the strategy of contingencies. That is, "reward" yourself with some pleasant activity after you've completed the task. For example, you might tell yourself, "After I return that phone call, I can take my coffee break." This technique is the same that parents use when they want their children to complete their homework. The children who get to watch television after their homework is done are usually more efficient at completing it than are those who don't have such a restriction. When you use this strategy on yourself, you might be surprised at how effective it is. The bonus is the relief you feel when the obligation is no longer hanging over you.

The strategies described here also apply to other self-defeating failures to act, such as getting exercise, getting medical checkups, and talking to someone about something that is uncomfortable but important. The main goal is to cut through your inner brat's excuses and whining.

In a way, self-defeating failures to act are not as difficult to overcome as are some of the feelings and behaviors related to desire and anger. It takes more mental strength to restrain yourself from doing something than it does to force yourself to do something. For example, when you're tired and you'd really like a glass of wine but resist the urge, you don't necessarily feel better right away. On the other hand, when you're tired and you force yourself to go for a walk, you often do feel better.

Therefore, if you're trying to decide where to begin taming your inner brat and you're not sure how much energy you'll have, pick something like procrastination or exercise. You'll feel the benefits immediately. From there, you can move on to working on your anger or addictive behaviors. It doesn't really matter where you begin. As the Nike slogan says, "Just do it." You won't regret it.

Conclusion

If you identified with many of the examples in this book, you're not alone. These examples represent the common types of problems that most people have. In my twenty-seven years as a clinical psychologist, I have heard similar stories day after day. Each person's situation is unique, but human nature is universal. Impulse control is a problem that goes back to biblical times and will likely be with us for many generations to come.

I hope that this book has given you some insight into how your mind works. The inner brat part of your mind has the potential to sabotage your best efforts, but your rational side is well equipped to maintain a healthy balance.

You will never have complete control over all of your impulses—at least I hope you won't, because the positive side of impulsiveness is spontaneity and creativity. For that reason, you must keep a window open for whims and urges. Naturally, some counterproductive impulses will also leak through. But now that you have some tools to deal with them, you can minimize their negative impact. No longer will you have to feel at the mercy of your inner brat.

14

Now that I`ve Tamed My Own Inner Brat, What Do I Do about People Who Haven`t Tamed Theirs?

If you've followed the suggestions so far in this book, you are well on your way to taming your inner brat. You are becoming more patient and more productive. You are less apt to get angry or to give into temptation. That's the good news.

The bad news is that you still have to deal with other people's inner brats. According to recent research, bratty behavior is all around us, and is not likely to diminish any time soon.

Rudeness and Rage Are All around Us

Rudeness, road rage, air rage, desk rage and myriad other rages are reported daily in the news, and have captured the attention of academic researchers. Here are some examples:

In January, 2002, the opinion organization Public Agenda conducted a large-scale survey, *Aggravating Circumstances: A Status Report on Rude-*

ness in America. Still reeling from September 11, the majority of those interviewed described society as more caring and supportive since the attacks on the U.S., but only 34% expected the changes to last. As for the respondents' overall impression of the degree of incivility in America, 88% said they often or sometimes encountered people who were rude or disrespectful.

More recently Public Agenda surveyed travel industry employees and passengers. The majority of respondents cited rudeness and bad behavior as major sources of stress and aggravation for both passengers and transportation workers. More than half of them also admitted being rude themselves.

Statistics from the Federal Aviation Association indicate that there are around 300 incidents of unruly passengers on American planes every year — almost double the number in 1995. And these include only people who have clearly violated laws. The Association of Flight Attendants claims that the actual number of disruptive passengers, including those that don't get reported, is closer to 4,000 per year.

Customer service has become so problematic that there are now websites where people can vent and complain (e.g., complaintstation.com) and where service workers can rant about rude and demanding customers (e.g., customerssuck.com).

Several studies show that incivility is a growing problem in the workplace. Dr. Lilia Cortina and her colleagues[21] at the University of Michigan surveyed 1,180 public-sector employees and found that 71% of them had experienced incivility from coworkers in the previous five years. Dr. Christine Pearson[22] at the University of North Carolina and her colleagues analyzed data from 775 workers. More than half said they lost work time thinking about past and future interactions with rude office mates, 37% admitted that their commitment to their employer had declined, and 46% considered changing jobs because of unpleasant coworkers.

Aggression and boorishness on the roads is well documented. Every day scores of news stories of road rage are published. At an international meeting of road safety experts in April, 2004, it was estimated that 1.2 million lives are lost each year because of intentional aggression or violation of road rules. In the USA alone, according to the National Highway Traffic Safety Administration, 17,000 people are killed in alcohol-related traffic accidents every year — accidents that probably wouldn't have happened had the drivers not been drunk behind the wheel.

In children's community sports, incivility and violence by parents has become epidemic. Several states have passed laws to protect sports officials from threats and assaults, and hundreds of communities have found it necessary to compile and enforce codes of conduct, because parents cannot seem to control their behavior on the sidelines. A tragic example is the case of Thomas Junta, who, at his son's hockey practice, beat another parent to death.

Schools are having problems as well. Disrespectful students disrupt classes and interfere with learning. Mindful of potentially litigious parents, teachers and principals tend to under-discipline rather than risk being sued. Both teachers and parents report that discipline and behavior problems are serious and pervasive.[23]

It is thus evident that on a regular basis you're going to encounter other people's inner brats, especially the inconsiderate or hostile variety.

What's more, such behavior is apt to push your emotional hot buttons. When a store clerk or a waitress seems to deliberately do something to make you mad, or when a coworker makes an insulting remark, it is hard to keep your own inner brat from lashing out in return.

Other People's Bad Habits

Most of the time other people's bad habits do not affect you personally. If they drink too much, or spend too much money or procrastinate important tasks — these are of little consequence to you. The exception, of course, is with people with whom you live or work closely. In that case, their bad habits can have a major impact on you. It's not easy to ignore a spouse's extravagant spending if you are constantly behind in your bills. It's almost impossible to disregard a coworker's procrastination when you depend on that person's work in order to complete your own.

When other people close to you fail to tame their inner brats your patience is seriously challenged. You may find it difficult to understand why they can't just "shape up," especially when you don't share their particular bad habit. As you become more annoyed with their lack of self-discipline, your own inner brat may emerge in the form of the Eruptor, the Smolderer, the Whiner or the Martyr. (See Chapter 8.)

How to Prevent Other People's Inner Brats from Triggering Your Own

Temporary irritations

When you encounter rude or inconsiderate people in traffic, in stores or in offices that you visit, the best thing to do is ignore the rude behavior. Why let their inner brat cause you grief when you'll be out of the situation within a short time? This is the time to ask yourself, "Will this matter in a week . . . or in a half an hour, even?"

Another approach is to respond in an extra polite or considerate manner. This gives you a feeling of control over the situation. You are being polite not because you have to, but because you choose to. Your gracious behavior often has the effect of disarming the other person's rudeness, as in the following example:

In his book, *Life Doesn't Get Any Better than This*,[24] Robert Alper describes his experience while driving on the highway one evening. He had just passed a car that had slowed down suddenly in front of him. The other driver became irate and started to tailgate and gesture rudely. This went on for several miles. When he noticed the other driver following him off the exit toward the tollbooth, Alper writes, "I took a final look at the grim face in the rearview mirror, and then I did it. I paid his toll." Later the other driver caught up with him, but this time he gestured apologetically.

More enduring inner brats

There's no escaping some people's inner brats. You may have to work with them, serve on committees with them, or even live with them. But just because they lose their cool, doesn't mean you have to. Here are some tips:

- **Detach yourself emotionally.** One of the quickest ways to do this is to imagine that you're watching a movie of the person. Observe his body language; listen to his tone of voice. See if you can decipher his inner brat's persona. If the bratty behavior is typical of this person, remind yourself, "Of course he over-reacted. What else would I expect from him?"

- **Determine who owns the problem.** If the other person is yelling at you or being hypercritical, ask yourself whether you are truly deserving of such a dressing-down. If you feel embarrassed by her rant, keep in mind that such behavior reflects more about her than about you.

- **Protect your own emotional hot buttons.** You know what sets you off. Be prepared. But this time, instead of anticipating how awful it's going to be to deal with the other person, devise a strategy. Make a plan. Think of it as a game. For example, say to yourself, "I wonder how long it will take John to start challenging everything I say. I'll give him ten minutes . . . no, make that five." Such an attitude not only helps keep you calm; it also gives you something else to do besides bracing yourself for criticism.

- **One of the most effective ways to respond to sarcasm is to utter a statement of agreement.** Rehearse some statements that you can use when someone's hostile inner brat gets to you. Let's say your sister-in-law always makes catty remarks, which leave you feeling defenseless and angry. Instead of arguing or walking away, agree with her: e.g., "Yes, Mary, I see what you mean. I really do have poor taste in wallpaper." This will stop her inner brat in its tracks, since you've taken away its power.

- **Disarm the other person's inner brat by giving it what it wants before it demands it.** This takes a bit of practice, but it can be quite effective. For example, let's say you work with someone with a strong Exhibitionist inner brat. Exhibitionists like to have attention. They brag or gossip or dramatize everything. Most people try to avoid giving the Exhibitionist any more attention. But I'm recommending that you do the opposite. Before your coworker with the Exhibitionist inner brat even starts talking, give him a compliment or ask his advice. "Isn't this encouraging his inner brat?" you might ask. No, because you're doing it on your terms, not his. You'll find that once you give him your attention, he's had his "fix" and he'll back off. Note that this approach does not help tame the other person's inner brat; it only makes it less irritating for you.

Other people's bad habits that affect you

As stated earlier, other people's bad habits can affect everyone around them. You can't control their behavior, but you need not be worn down by it. Instead of investing your energy into trying to control their behavior or getting mad, make decisions and plans for how you are going to get on with your life in spite of their problems. Here's what to do:

- **Try to limit the degree to which you must depend on the other person.** For example, if your spouse has promised to fix something at home but hasn't got around to it for several months (or years!) hire someone to do it, especially if you are greatly inconvenienced by the situation. Similarly, if you find yourself waiting for someone who is always late to pick you up, consider finding alternate transportation. And decide in advance how long you will be willing to wait for the other person. Be prepared to leave if the other person doesn't show up by that time.

- **Have realistic expectations.** You have no control over the other person's inner brat, nor over the other person's behavior. Spendthrifts spend money. Alcoholics drink. Smokers smoke. Threats and scoldings are not only ineffective at making the other person change; they also bring out your own inner brat. The best you can do is figure out how (or if) you are going to live with the problem. Make a plan and stick to it. So, for example, if your spouse spends more money than you have coming in, decide how to separate your finances so that your own credit rating stays intact. If your roommate smokes and this is offensive to you, find another roommate.

- **View the problem in perspective.** In her advice column, Ann Landers used to reply to people who complained about spouses' bad habits or vices, "Ask yourself: Would you be better off with him or without him?" Sometimes your own inner brat can magnify a small problem such that it becomes an unnecessary focus of your life. This is the time to say to your inner brat, "Get over it."

- **On the other hand,** there are times when the other person's bad habits are so pervasive that they cannot be ignored, minimized or endured. In such cases you may have to take the step of reporting the problem if it's at work, or seeking legal or psychological help if it involves your personal life.

While you're on the lookout for other people's inner brats, don't lose sight of your own. Recall (from Chapter 3) that we tend to give ourselves more slack and to be more harshly critical of others. In the Public Agenda survey described earlier, 88% of those interviewed said they had encountered rude behavior in others. But here's another statistic that I haven't mentioned yet: only 41% admitted being rude themselves. This means that a lot of people grossly underestimate the extent to which they offend others. Let's hope you're not one of them.

Just to be on the safe side, make a point of cultivating patience, civility and consideration of others. There are clear advantages to taking charge of your own inner brat even when those around you do not control theirs. First, you are calmer and more rational. You have the upper hand in the situation. Second, there are minimal aftereffects. You are better able to let go of the frustration and get on with your life. Third, when you treat others in a civil manner, you tend to disarm their inner brat, such that their behavior improves as well - at least temporarily.

But the most important advantage of controlling your own inner brat is that your outlook on life will become more positive. No longer preoccupied with what's wrong with other people or with what you can't have, you are better able to focus on what's going well. Research shows that people who focus on positive aspects of themselves and their world, are happier and more optimistic in general, regardless of their health, financial situation, education or physical attractiveness.

So here's to taming your inner brat; to not trying to tame anyone else's; and to turning your attention to what's going right in your life.

Notes

1. Jack Trimpey, *Rational Recovery: The New Cure for Substance Addiction* (New York: Pocket Books, 1996).

2. John Leo, *Two Steps Ahead of the Thought Police* (New York: Simon & Shuster, 1994), 50.

3. The "Twinkie defense" refers to a 1978 murder case in which San Francisco City Supervisor Dan White climbed through a basement window of City Hall and shot and killed Mayor George Moscone and City Supervisor Harvey Milk. At his trial, a psychiatrist for the defense testified that White had acted under diminished mental capacity because of depression exacerbated by eating junk food. Contrary to media reports that the psychiatrist claimed the junk food caused White's depression, he actually said that White's recent junk-food habit only reflected his depression.

4. Charles L. Whitfield, *Healing the Child Within* (Deerfield Beach, Fla.: Health Communications, 1987).

5. Ibid.

6. CAT scan: Computerized axial tomography, an advanced x-ray technique for viewing the brain; MRI: Magnetic resonant imaging, an advanced brain-imaging technique that uses electromagnetic signals to show the brain's structure and functioning.

7. William Shakespeare, *Hamlet*, Act II.

8. Trimpey, *Rational Recovery*.

9. Lawrence H. Diller, *Running on Ritalin: A Physician Reflects on Children, Society and Performance in a Pill* (New York: Bantam Doubleday Dell, 1998).

10. Daniel P. Goleman, *Emotional Intelligence: Why It Can Matter More Than IQ for Character, Health and Lifelong Achievement* (New York: Bantam Books, 1997).

11. Christopher Lasch, *The Culture of Narcissism: American Life in an Age of Diminishing Expectations* (New York: W. W. Norton, 1979).

12. *The Guardian*, 29 February 2000. Donna MacLean's patent application was submitted in protest of the mass patenting of human genes by science and big business.

13. Robert Bly, *The Sibling Society* (New York: Random House, Vintage Books, 1997).

14. David Burns, *Feeling Good: The New Mood Therapy* (New York: William Morrow, 1980).

15. Roy F. Baumeister, Todd F. Heatherton, and Dianne M. Tice, *Losing Control: How and Why People Fail at Self-Regulation* (San Diego, Calif.: Academic Press, 1994). See also M. Muraven and R. Baumeister, "Self-Regulation and Depletion of Limited Resources: Does Self-Control Resemble a Muscle?" *Psychological Bulletin* 126, no. 2 (2000): 247–259.

16. C. P. Herman and D. Mack, "Restrained and Unrestrained Eating," *Journal of Personality* 43 (1975): 647–660.

17. Daniel M. Wegner, D. J. Schneider, S. R. Carter III, and L. White, "Paradoxical Effects of Thought Suppression," *Journal of Personality and Social Psychology* 58 (1987): 409–418.

18. Mark Muraven, Dianne M. Tice, and Roy Baumeister, "Self-Control as Limited Resource: Regulatory Depletion Patterns," *Journal of Personality and Social Psychology* 74 (1998): 774–789.

19. Mark Muraven, R. L. Collins, and K. Nienhaus, "Self-Control and Alcohol Restraint: A Test of the Self-Control Strength Model" (unpublished manuscript).

20. Goleman, *Emotional Intelligence*.

21 Cortina, L.M., Magley, V.J., Williams, J.H., Langout, R.D., Incivility in the workplace: incidence and impact. *Journal of Occupational Health Psychology*, *Vol.* 6, 64–80, 2001.

22 Pearson, C., Andersson, L., & Porath, C. 2000. Assessing and attacking workplace incivility. Organizational Dynamics , 29(2): 123-137.

23 *Teaching Interrupted: Do Discipline Policies in Today's Public Schools Foster the Common Good?* Prepared by Public Agenda with support from Common Good, 2004

24 Alper, Robert A., *Life Doesn't Get Any Better Than This*, Ligouri, Missouri, Liguori/Triumph 1996.

Index

A

abandonment, 4, 5

activity level, 201–3

addiction, 16–17, 43–44, 47, 69

addictive behaviors, 8, 24–29, 68–69, 125, 173, 180–81, 196, 232–33. *See also* alcoholism; all-or-nothing thinking; sexual infidelity; smoking

addictive voice, 16, 29, 44, 68–69

Addictive Voice Recognition Technique, 68

ADHD, 78–81, 85–86

Adult ego state, 17, 63–64, 72, 75, 123

-aholic (suffix), 43

Alcoholics Anonymous, 16, 43, 198–99

alcoholism, 16–17, 42–44, 68–69, 134, 145, 194, 196–99, 218, 232–33. *See also* addiction; addictive behaviors

all-or-nothing thinking, 154, 188–89, 197–99, 200

American Psychiatric Association, 79

American Psychological Association, 166, 231

Americans with Disabilities Act, 44

anger
  "calming" strategy for, 209–13, 235–36
  uncontrolled, 4, 6–8, 32–35, 66, 168–69, 172, 193, 233–37
  unexpressed, 32–33
  See also overreactions

archetypes, Jung's, 62–63, 72–73

assumptions, 65–66, 155–56, 159–61. *See also* cognitive distortions

attention deficit disorder, 78–81, 85–86

attention deficit hyperactivity disorder, 78–81, 85–86

attention span, short, 85–89

attributions
  bias in, 40–42, 176
  process of, 38–42, 65–66

authority, respect for, 109–10, 112

awfulizing (irrational exaggerations), 60, 68, 155, 160, 195, 222–23, 228, 238–39

B

baby boomers, 103–6

Baumeister, Roy, 184–85

"Beast," the, 16–17, 18, 69

Beck, Aaron T., 151, 153

behaviors
  bratty, 19–20, 24–35, 52, 232–37
  irrational, 7
  origin of, 103–11
  passive aggressive, 35, 234–35
  self-defeating, 30–32, 241–43
  See also addictive behaviors; bratty feelings; bratty thoughts; inner brat

beliefs, irrational, 67–68, 160

Berne, Eric, 17, 18, 63–64, 72, 74–75, 83, 123

biases, 40–42, 176

"Bill of No Rights," 229–30

Bly, Robert, 112

brain, function of, 56–57. *See also* mind

brat, defined, 1, 7–8, 91. *See also* inner brat

34211748R00156

Made in the USA
Lexington, KY
02 August 2014